Morality and Rules of Happiness

Thomas Foster

Morality and Rules of Happiness

LM Publishers

Introduction

The purpose of these papers is to show how rules of conduct may be established on a scientific basis for those who regard the so-called religious basis as unsound. I shall follow chiefly the teachings of one who has inculcated in their best and purest form the scientific doctrines of morality, and may be regarded as head, if not founder, of that school of philosophy which, on purely scientific grounds, sets happiness as the test of duty the measure of moral obligation. To Mr. Herbert Spencer we owe, I take it, the fullest and clearest answer to the melancholy question, "Is Life Worth Living?" whether asked whiningly, as in the feeble lamentations of such folk as Mr. Mallock, or gloomily and sternly, as in the Promethean groans of Carlyle. The doctrine that happiness is to be sought for one's self (but as a duty to others as well as to self), that the happiness of others is to be sought as a duty (to one's self as well as to them) happiness as a means, happiness as the chief end such has been the outcome of the much-maligned philosophy of Mr. Herbert Spencer, such has been the lesson resulting from his pursuance of what he himself describes as his " ultimate purpose, lying behind all proximate purposes," that of "finding for the principles of right and wrong, in conduct at large, a scientific basis."

If I can help to bring this noble and beautiful doctrine for noble and beautiful even those must admit it to be who deny its truth before the many who regard Herbert Spencer's teachings with fear and trembling, not knowing what they are, I shall be content. But I would advise all, who have time, to read the words of the master himself. Apart from the great doctrines which they convey, they are delightful reading, clear and simple in language, graceful and dignified in tone, almost as worthy to be studied as examples of force and clearness in exposition as for that which nevertheless constitutes their real value the pure and beautiful moral doctrines which they offer to those over whom current creeds have lost their influence.

Let me hope that none will be deterred from following this study, by the inviting aspect of the moral rules advanced by the great modern teacher even as in past times men were anxious, or even angry, when another teacher showed more consideration for human weaknesses than had seemed right to the men of older times. I will not ask here whether doctrines of repellent aspect are likely to be more desirable than those which are more benignantly advanced. It suffices that with many the former now exert no influence, whether they should do so or not. So that, as far as these (for whom I am chiefly writing) are concerned, all must admit the truth of what Mr. Spencer says respecting the benefits to be derived from presenting moral rule under that attractive aspect which it has when undisturbed by superstition and asceticism. To close these introductory remarks by a quotation from the charming pages of his "Data of Ethics": "If a father, sternly enforcing numerous commands, some needful and some needless, adds to his severe control a behavior wholly unsympathetic if his children have to take their pleasures by stealth, or, when timidly looking up from their play, ever meet a cold glance, or more frequently a frown, his government will inevitably be disliked, if not hated; and the aim will be to evade it as much as possible. Contrariwise, a father who, equally firm in maintaining restraints needful for the well-being of his children, or the well-being of other persons, not only avoids needless restraints, but, giving his sanction to all legitimate gratifications, and providing the means for them, looks on at their gambols with an approving smile, can scarcely fail to gain an influence which, no less efficient for the time being, will also be permanently efficient. The controls of such two fathers symbolize the controls of morality as it is and morality as it should be."

Chap.1
Conduct and Duty

Morality relates to those parts of our conduct of which it can be said that they are right or wrong. Under the general subject conduct, then, morality is included as a part. On regarding the word "duty" as implying all that we ought to do and all that we ought to avoid, we may say that duty is a part of conduct. All actions which are not purposeless may be regarded as included under the word "conduct," as well as some which, though purposeless at the time, result from actions originally done with purpose until a fixed habit had been acquired. But only those actions which we consider good or bad are referred to when we speak of duty; and the principles of what we call morality relate only to these.

Here, however, we have already recognized a connection between duty and conduct generally, which should show all who are familiar with scientific methods that morality cannot properly be discussed in its scientific aspect without discussing conduct at large. Every student of science knows that, rightly to consider a part, he must consider the whole to which it belongs. In every department of science this general law holds, though it is not always recognized. No scientific subject has ever been properly dealt with until it has been considered in its relations to its surroundings as well as separately. Even in matters not usually considered from a scientific stand-point the same law holds. To go no further than our own pages, the writer who is dealing with the question "How to get strong?" would not consider how the arms are to be strengthened without duly considering that the arms are part of the body, their exercise related to the exercise of other portions, their development associated with the development of other limbs, with the action of other parts of the body, with the regimen proper for the whole frame.

It may not by many be regarded as a fault of most systems of morality that they overlook the necessary connection between conduct in general and conduct as guided by moral considerations. For many are content to regard moral laws as existing apart from any of the results of experience whether derived from individual conduct, the conduct of men generally, or conduct as seen among creatures of all orders. With many, morality is looked upon as a whole the whole duty of man not as a part of conduct. They even consider that moral obligations must be weakened when their dependence on conduct in general is insisted upon. Moral rules, with them, are right in themselves and of necessity and whether inculcated by extra-human authority, or enjoined by law, or perceived intuitively, are open neither to inquiry nor objection. Clearly if this were so, morality would not be a fitting subject for the scientific method. Its rules would be determinable apart from the discussion of evidence based on experience, whether observational or experimental. I do not here inquire whether this view is right or wrong. Later on it will fall into my plan to do so. At present I only note that we are considering our subject from the stand-point of those who desire to view morality in its scientific aspect. For them it is essential that, as conduct in general includes conduct depending on duty, the discussion of questions of duty cannot be complete or satisfactory unless it is conducted with due reference to the whole of which this subject forms a part.

If any doubt could exist in the mind of the student on this point, it should be removed when he notes that it is impossible to draw any sharply defined line between duty and the rest of conduct not depending on considerations of duty. Not only are those actions which under particular circumstances seem absolutely indifferent found under other circumstances to be right or wrong and not indifferent, not only do different persons form different ideas as to what part of conduct is indifferent or otherwise, but one and the same person in different parts of his life finds that he draws different distinctions between conduct in general and conduct to be guided by moral considerations. In the evolution of conduct in a nation, in a town, in a family, or in the individual man, the line separating conduct regarded as indifferent from conduct regarded as right or wrong is ever varying in position sometimes tending to include among actions indifferent those which had been judged bad or good, oftener tending to show right or wrong in conduct which had been judged indifferent.

If moral laws, then, are to be established on a scientific basis, it is essential that conduct at large should be carefully considered; and not conduct only as it is seen in man, but as it is seen in animals of every grade. Thus and thus only can the evolution of conduct be rightly studied; by the study of the evolution of conduct only can the scientific distinction between right and wrong be recognized; from and out of this distinction only can moral laws be established for those with whom the authoritative enunciation of such laws has no longer the weight it once had, those who find no other inherent force in moral statutes than they derive as resulting from experience, and who reject as unreasonable all belief in the intuitive recognition of laws of morality.

We proceed, then, to consider the evolution of conduct in the various types of animal life, from the lowest upward to man. — *Knowledge*.

Chap.2
The Evolution of conduct

I

As structures are evolved, so are the functions which structures subserve. And as the functions of the body are evolved, so are those combinations of bodily actions evolved which we include under the general term conduct. We are considering the functions of the body when we are inquiring into such actions of the various structures internal and external as involve internal processes, simple or complex. But, when we begin to consider combinations of actions externally manifested, we are dealing with *conduct*—except only in the case of such actions as are independent of control.

But at the outset of the evolution of conduct even this distinction is scarcely to be recognized. Every external combination of actions is in the lower types of animal life a part of conduct at least of such conduct as is possible in the lowest orders of creatures. Evolution of conduct begins with the gradual development of purpose where at first actions were random and aimless. The *Amœba* wanders from place to place, not by the action of limbs, but by a process which may be called *diffluence*. In so doing it may come into the neighborhood of objects fit to form its food; these it enwraps, and absorbing what is digestible rejects the rest. Or its wanderings may lead it into the way of some creature by which it is itself absorbed and digested. There may be some higher law than chance guiding the movements of such creatures; but so far as can be judged this is not the case. In other words there is but the suspicion of something like *conduct* in the actions of the Amœba. Among other creatures belonging to the same kingdom, but higher in type, we find actions so much better adjusted, that, though even yet we cannot recognize such evidence of purpose as enables us to describe their actions as conduct, we yet see in their adjustment to certain ends the development of something akin to conduct. The actions seem guided by what mimics purpose if it is not purpose itself.

Now, we note that with the improved adjustment of actions comes an increase in the average duration of life, or rather in the proportion of this average to the length of life possible among these several creatures.

So when we pass to higher and higher orders of animals, we find in every case among the lower types irregular and seemingly purposeless actions, while among the higher we find actions better adjusted to the surroundings. And, again, we note that, where the combination of actions, or what we may now call the conduct, is not adjusted to the environment, the creatures' chances of life are small, great numbers dying for each whose life approaches the average duration. An improved adjustment of conduct to environment increases the chances of survival, many attaining and some passing the average of longevity in their particular type or order.

Now, structural development is guided by the fitness or unfitness of particular proportions in such and such structures for the great life-struggle in which all animal life is constantly engaged; and functional development is guided by the corresponding fitness or unfitness of such and such functional activities. Just as certainly the development of conduct in all orders of living creatures is guided by the fitness or unfitness of such and such combinations of external actions for the constant life-contest.

We might find illustrations of this in every kingdom, sub-kingdom, order, and type, of animal life. Let us, however, content ourselves by noting it in man.

In the lower races of man as at present existing, and in still greater degree among the lower races when the human race as a whole was lower, we see that the adjustments of external actions to obtain food, to provide shelter against animate and inanimate enemies, and otherwise to support or to defend life, are imperfect and irregular. The savage of the lowest type is constantly exposed to the risk of losing his life either through hunger or cold, or through storm, or from attacks against which he has not made adequate provision. He neither foresees nor remembers, and his conduct is correspondingly aimless and irregular. The least provident, or rather the most improvident, perish in greatest numbers. Hence there is an evolution of conduct from irregularity and aimlessness by slow degrees toward the regularity and adaptation of aims to ends, seen in advancing civilization. The ill-adjusted conduct which diminishes the chances of life dies out in the struggle for life, to make way for the better-adjusted conduct by which the chances of life are increased. The process is as certain in its action as the process of structural evolution. In either process we see multitudinous individual exceptions. Luck plays its part in individual cases; but inexorable law claims its customary rule over averages. In the long run conduct best adapted and adjusted to environment is developed at the expense of conduct less suitable to the surroundings.

With man, as with all orders of animals, conduct which tends to increase the duration of life prevails over conduct having an opposite tendency. Wherefore, remembering the ever-varying conditions under which life is passed, the evolution of conduct means not only the development of well-adjusted actions, but the elaboration of conduct to correspond with those diverse and multitudinous conditions.

To these considerations we may add that the evolution of conduct not only tends necessarily to increased length of life (necessarily, because shortening of life means the diminution of such conduct as tends to shorten life), but it results in increased breadth of life, and (in the highest animal) in increased depth of life also. It is manifest that, in the elaboration of activities by which length of life is increased, breadth of life is increased *pari passu*. For these activities maybe said 'to constitute breadth of life. Passing over the numerous illustrations which might be drawn from the lower orders of animal life, we recognize in man a vast increase in the breadth of life as we pass from the limited orders of activity constituting the life of the savage to the multiplied and complex activities involved in civilized life. Increased depth of life we recognize only (but we recognize it clearly) in the most advanced races of that animal which not only thinks and reasons but reflects.

We find, then, that the evolution of conduct is not only accompanied by increased fullness of life, but is to be estimated by such increase. We do not say that that conduct is good in relation to the individual which increases and that conduct bad which diminishes the fullness of individual life in the individual. We assert, for the present, only what observation shows—that conduct of the former kind is favored (other things equal), and therefore developed, in the life-struggle, while conduct of the latter sort tends to disappear as evolution proceeds.

Thus far we have only considered conduct in relation to individual life. We have still to consider the evolution of conduct as related to the life of the species.

In considering the evolution of structures and functions we have not only to consider the influence of the struggle for individual existence, but also the effects of the contest in which each race as a whole is engaged—and to do this we have to consider, first, those circumstances which affect the propagation of the race; secondly, the relation of the individuals of the race to their fellows; thirdly, the relations of the race as a whole to other races. Something akin to this must be done in considering the evolution of conduct. We have seen how modes of conduct which favor the continued existence of the individual are developed at the expense of modes of conduct having an opposite tendency. These last die out, because the individuals of the race who act in these ways die out. But it is obvious that conduct will be equally apt to die out which tends to prevent or limit the adequate renewal of the race from generation to generation. It is equally obvious that whatever conduct causes contests (whether for life or subsistence) within the race or species, tends to the elimination of members of the race, and so diminishes the chances of the race in the struggle for existence with other races. Lastly, the relations of a race to surrounding races are manifestly of importance in the evolution of conduct, seeing that conduct will equally tend to be diminished whether it is unfavorable to the existence of the race in which it is prevalent, or simply unfavorable to the separate existence of an individual member of the race.

Now, with regard to conduct affecting the propagation of a race, we find that, like conduct affecting individual life, it has been developed from what can hardly be called conduct at all in the lowest grades of life to fully developed conduct, with elaborate adaptation of means to ends in the highest. In the lowest forms of life, propagation proceeds by mere division and subdivision, not depending so far as can be judged on any power of controlling the process, which such creatures may possess. In fact, the *Protozoa* multiply by dividing. We have to pass over many grades of life before we reach such imperfect care for propagation of the race as we find among those orders of fish in which the male keeps watch and ward over the eggs. Still higher must we pass before we find any trace of affection for the young, and higher yet before we see care given to feed and protect and keep the young till they are able to provide for themselves.

This brings us in fact very near to the human race, which, in its lowest races, is distinguished from other animals chiefly by the length of time during which it feeds, protects, and trains its young. In the higher human races all these processes are conducted with greater care and elaboration; more varied wants are considered and attended to, more elaborately varied means are used for the purpose. It is easily seen how such conduct by aiding the development of the race aids the development of the conduct itself by which that result is favored. Among those members of a race in whom the proper race-propagating conduct is not adequately shown, propagation proceeds less effectively—which is the same as saying that, relatively, such conduct itself must be diminishing.

This conclusion is not inconsistent, as at first sight it might appear, with the fact that mere numerical increase of propagation, though it means increase in quantity of life, is not always or even generally a proof of the growth of the race in what may be called race-vitality. Here as elsewhere adaptation of means to ends has to be considered, and that kind of conduct by which such adaptation is secured has the best chances of development in the long run. Let us, for instance, take an illustration from civilized life: An early marriage between two persons, careless alike of present duties and future difficulties, seems at first to tend directly to the increase of carelessness and thoughtlessness; for from such a union there will probably come into existence more than the average number of offspring, repeating in greater or less degree the weak characters of their parents: the totality of life characterized by undesirable qualities and conduct will thus be increased, and increased in a greater ratio than the totality of prudent, steady, and thoughtful life, by a well-considered union and well-judged conduct thereafter. Yet in the long run the result proves usually otherwise. (We consider only average results.) The larger number of offspring of inferior qualities receive less care and inferior training; so that for them there is greater probability either of early death or of defective adult life. The parents suffer also in the struggle thus brought on them, for which they are ill-fitted. A diminished amount of life is likely to result, and (taking the average of many cases) probably does result; while certainly there is diminished life-quality. Hence results a correspondingly diminished amount and influence of the inferior kind of conduct shown by thoughtlessness or carelessness about life's duties. On the other hand, the well-judged and not too hasty union of two care-taking persons, though it may add a smaller number of individual lives to the life of the race, adds better and more enduring life, life more likely to maintain and sustain the qualities of the parents, giving therefore to these qualities in the race at once more stability and wider influence. In other words, the qualities best suited for the propagation of the race, and best suited for the race, will on the average be developed, while qualities having opposite tendencies will either be eliminated, or though they may remain will occupy a lower place and have diminished influence on the fortunes of the race—a circumstance tending of itself still further to their eventual elimination.

But, within a race and in the relations of the race to other races, there are causes which influence the evolution of conduct. Members of a race fight out the contest for existence not alone but more or less in the presence of their fellows and in the presence of members of other races. Each individual in providing for his own wants or for his own defense affects more or less others, either of his own race or of other races, in their efforts to defend or sustain *their* lives. Very often, as Mr. Herbert Spencer quaintly puts it, "a successful adjustment by one creature involves an unsuccessful adjustment made by another creature, either of the same kind or of a different kind." The lion and the lamb, for instance, already anticipate the millennium; but the lion adjusts matters so much more successfully than the lamb as to take the outside place; the lamb lies down with the lion, but—inside. Among all races, herbivorous as well as carnivorous, similar relations exist. The more vigorous get the better food, food which the weaker contend for in vain or have to resign, when obtained, to superior strength. Within one and the same race there is still the same law. The stronger monopolize, if they can, the feeding-grounds of the race. The weaker, whether originally so, or become so through age or disease, succumb in greater numbers than the stronger in the struggle for existence. Only, while the death of those weak through age does not affect the evolution of the race, the greater mortality among those originally weaker than the rest modifies the race-qualities.

In these contests conduct plays an important part. Unnecessary contests involve unnecessary risks. That conduct must prevail best in the long run, and therefore that conduct must eventually be evolved and developed, by which adjustments for the advantage of one creature do not needlessly interfere with adjustments for the advantage of other creatures. If we imagine a carnivorous animal carefully limiting his search for animal food to his requirements, not killing where there was no occasion, and keeping carefully all food he had once obtained, we see that his chances in the life-struggle would be better than those of a carnivore of the same race who killed whenever he got the chance. It would be more the interest of other creatures (as for instance those who wanted the same sort of food) to eliminate the carnivore of the latter sort, than to remove the more prudent member of the race. In the long run this would tell even among the lower animals. But, as we approach the relations of men to men and men to animals, we see more obviously how conduct in which the interests or the wants of others are considered is safer in the long run, more conducive (in hundreds of ways more or less complex) to prolonged existence, than conduct in which those interests and wants are neglected. Hence there will be a tendency, acting slowly but surely, to the evolution of conduct of the former kind. More of those whose conduct is of that character, or approaches that character, will survive in each generation, than of those whose conduct is of an opposite character.

The difference may be slight, and therefore the effect in a single generation, or even in several, may also be slight; but in the long run the law must tell. Conduct of the sort least advantageous will tend to die out, because those showing it will have relatively inferior life-chances.

Mr. Spencer seems to me to leave his argument a little incomplete just here. For, though he shows that conduct avoiding harm to others, in all races, must tend to make the totality of life larger, this in reality is insufficient. He is dealing with the evolution of conduct. Now, to take a concrete example, those of the hawk tribe who left little birds alone, except when they had no other way to keep themselves alive but by capturing and killing them, would help to increase the totality of life, by leaving more birds to propagate their kind than would be left if a more wholesale slaughter were carried out. But this of itself would not tend to develop that moderation of hawk character which we have imagined. The creatures helped in the life-struggle would not be the hawks (so far as this particular increase in the totality of life was concerned), but the small birds; and the only kind of moderation or considerateness encouraged would be shown in a lessening of that extreme diffidence, that desire to withdraw themselves wholly from hawk society, which we recognize among small birds. But if it be shown that the more wildly rapacious hawks stand a greater chance of being destroyed than those of a more moderate character, then we see that such moderation and steadiness of character are likely to be developed and finally established as a characteristic of the more enduring races of hawks. And similarly in other such cases.

It is, however, in the development of conduct in the higher races only, that this comparatively elaborate law of evolution is clearly recognized. Among savage races we still see apparent exceptions to the operation of the rule. Individuals and classes and races distinguished by ferocity and utter disregard of the "adjustments" of others, whether of their own race or of different races, seem to thrive well enough, better even than the more moderate and considerate. Forces really are at work tending to eliminate the more violent and greedy; but they are not obvious. As society advances, however, even this seeming success of the rapacious is found to diminish, though as yet there has been no race or society from which it has been actually eliminated. Conduct which is imperfect, conduct characterized by antagonisms between groups and antagonisms between members of the same group, tends to be more and more reduced in amount, by the failure or by the elimination of those who exhibit such conduct.

What is regarded as gallant daring in one generation is scorned as ferocity in a later one, resisted as rapacious wrong-doing yet later, and later still is eliminated either by death or nearly as effectually (when indirect as well as direct consequences are considered) by imprisonment.

As violence dies out, and as war diminishes—which usually is but violence manifested on a larger scale the kind of conduct toward which processes of evolution appear to tend, "that perfect adjustment of acts to ends in maintaining individual life and rearing new individuals, which is effected by each without hindering others from effecting like perfect adjustments," will be approached. How nearly it will ever be attained by any human race—*quien sabe?*

One further consideration, and we have done with the evolution of conduct, the right understanding of which is essential to the scientific study of conduct. The members of a society, while attending to adjustments necessary for their wants or interests, may not merely leave others free to make their adjustments also, but may help them in so doing. It is very obvious that conduct thus directed must tend to be developed. As Mr. Spencer says, such conduct facilitates the making of adjustments by each, and so increases the totality of the adjustments made, and serves to render the lives of all more complete. But besides this (as he should also have shown, since it is an essential part of the evolution argument), it tends to its own increase: for, being essentially mutual, conduct of this kind is a favorable factor in the life-struggle.

We have next to consider what, seeing thus the laws according to which conduct is evolved, we are to regard as good conduct and bad conduct.

II

In its scientific aspect, then, as indicated by processes of evolution, conduct is good in proportion as it tends to increase the quantity and the fullness of life, bad in proportion as it exerts a contrary influence. Conduct may tend to increase life in its fullness directly or indirectly, proximately or remotely; and again conduct may in one aspect increase, while in another aspect it may diminish, the fullness and quantity of life: but our definition of good and bad conduct is not affected by such considerations. Just as a knife may be a good knife for cutting bread, and a bad knife for cutting wood, just as a business transaction may be good in relation to some immediate purpose, yet bad when remoter effects are considered, so can we truly apply to conduct the terms *good* and *bad* in reference to one set of considerations, even though we may have to invert the terms when conduct is considered in reference to another set of considerations. But always, in its scientific aspect, conduct is to be regarded as good where it increases life or the fullness of life, and bad where it tends the contrary way.

When we separate conduct ethically indifferent from conduct in its strict ethical aspect, it is convenient to substitute for the words *good* and *bad* the words *right* and *wrong*. But the change is slighter than at first sight it appears. Indeed, the more carefully the question of rightness or wrongness—the question of *duty*—is considered, the more thoroughly does the kind of conduct judged to be morally indifferent merge into that which we regard as praiseworthy or censurable.

Taking first those parts of conduct which relate directly to the quantity or to the fullness of individual life, we find that while the terms good and bad are freely applied to them, and even the terms right and wrong, they are, for the most part, regarded as morally indifferent. When we say you *ought* to do this or to refrain from that, the idea of duty is often not really present, so long as the act in question relates to a man's own life or its fullness. Even when we use words of praise or censure in relation to such acts, they do not imply that a moral obligation has been discharged or neglected. The reason doubtless is that, as a rule, men need little encouragement to look after those parts of their conduct which affect themselves and their own interests. For it may be observed that where it is likely there may be want of due care or wisdom in such matters, there we find distinct exceptions to the general rule just indicated. So far as quantity and fullness of life are concerned, the man who crosses a crowded thoroughfare carelessly, he who neglects his business, and he who wears insufficient or unsuitable clothes in cold and wet weather, act with as little propriety in their adjustments as is shown by the man who steadily drinks intoxicating liquors. But while none preach such duties as caution in street-crossing, prudence and energy in business, and care about clothing, at least as duties morally obligatory, quite a number of persons preach against steady and heavy drinking as against a moral offense. The Bible, indeed, does not, though it has many a word of advice against wine-bibbing; yet even in the Bible we find evidence of the early existence of total abstainers, and it is altogether unlikely that those ancient Blue-Ribbonists omitted to recognize sinfulness in all who did not share their views and follow their practices. Here we find evidence of the law of moral philosophy that a system of ethics, with recognition of moral rightness and wrongness, only begins to be formed where the best conduct (so far as fullness of life is concerned) runs the chance, for whatever reason, of being neglected, and inferior conduct followed. In this case, the best conduct is apt to be neglected because the increased fullness of life to which it conduces is more remote than the temporary increase of life fullness to which inferior conduct tends.

Yet, speaking generally, it may be said that, as Mr. Herbert Spencer puts it: "The ethical judgments we pass on self-regarding acts are ordinarily little emphasized; partly because the promptings of the self-regarding desires, generally strong enough, do not need moral enforcement, and partly because the promptings of the other self-regarding desires, less strong, and often overridden, do need moral enforcement."

When we turn to the life-regarding actions of the second class, those which relate to the rearing of offspring, we no longer find the words good and bad, right and wrong, used with doubtful meaning. Here the question of duty is clearly recognized. The conduct of parents, who, by neglecting to provide for their children's wants in infancy, diminish their chances of full and active life, or of life itself, is called bad and wrong not solely or chiefly because it is not favorable to the increase of life, but as open to moral censure. In like manner, men blame as really wrong, not merely unwise or ill-adjusted, such conduct as tends to make the physical and mental training of children imperfect or inadequate.

Still clearer, however, is the use of the words right and wrong as applied to conduct by which men influence in various ways the lives of their fellows. Here the adjustments suitable for increasing the fullness of individual life, or for fostering the lives of offspring (alike in quantity and fullness), are often inconsistent with the corresponding adjustments of others. The development by evolution of conduct tending to the advancement of individual lives or lives of offspring would of itself tend constantly to acts inconsistent with the well-being or even with the existence of others, were it not for the development (also brought about, as we have seen, by processes of evolution) of conduct tending to the increase of the quantity and fullness of life in the community. But there arises a constant conflict between tendencies to opposite lines of conduct. It is so essential for the welfare of the community that tendencies to advance the life interests of self and children should be in due subordination (which is not the same thing, be it noticed, as complete subordination) to tendencies leading to the furtherance of the fullness of life in others, that rules of conduct toward others than self or children have to be emphatic and peremptory in tone. Hence it is, as Mr. Spencer justly remarks, that the words good and bad have come to be specially associated with acts which (respectively) *further* the complete living of others and acts which *obstruct* their complete living.

We approach now the heart of the matter. We have seen how conduct has been evolved in the various races of living creatures, from the lowest to man the highest. We have learned how closely related are men's ideas of good and bad to that which is the chief end of all conduct—the preservation and extension of life. And we have found that while the conception of rightness and wrongness is not very marked in relation to conduct affecting self-life, it becomes clear and obvious in relation to conduct affecting the life of offspring, and attains its greatest definiteness and as it were emphasis in its application to conduct affecting the lives of others. Where the rules determining right and wrong in regard to the life of self, of offspring, and of others, come into conflict, as they must until social relations become perfect, the right in regard to self mostly gives way to right in regard to offspring, and both usually give way to right in regard to the rest of humankind. But in Mr. Spencer's words (I quote them with emphasis, because he has been so preposterously and indeed wickedly charged with teaching a very different doctrine) "the conduct called good rises to the conduct conceived as best, when it fulfills all three classes of ends at the same time."

But now the vital question of all comes before us.

We conceive as good or bad such conduct as conduces or the reverse to life and the fullness of life, in self and others. But is conduct of the one kind really good or conduct of the other kind really bad? Though good or bad with reference to that particular end, and though held to be right or wrong because that end is actually in view among men, may not conduct be differently judged when the nature of that end is considered? In other words, the question comes before us, Is life worth living? We need not take either the optimist view, according to which life is very good, or the pessimist view, according to which it is very bad. But each one of us from his experience as regards his own life, and from his observation (often most misleading, however) on the lives of others, may be led to hold that on the whole life is good, or that on the whole it is bad. Of course, in the very theory of the evolution of conduct, or rather in the series of observed facts demonstrating the evolution of conduct, we see that life and the fullness of life are fought for throughout nature as if they were good. In the highest race the love of life in self, which assumes that the life of others also is good, has attained its highest expression. "Everything that a man has he will give for his life," is a rule established rather than shaken by exceptions and the attention directed to such exceptions. Yet the mere fact that life is fought for by all, and that the struggle for life has been so potent a factor in the development of life, does not in itself prove life to be an actual good. Death comes not alone. To creatures full of life death comes in company with pain and suffering. It may be these which move all living creatures to struggle for life, and not mere fear of death.

Now, to the question, Is life worth living? it would be impossible to give an answer that would suit all. Probably there have not been two human beings since the world was made who, could they express their precise opinion on this point, would give precisely the same answer. Many whose whole lives have been full of sorrow and trouble, who have had occasion many times to say that man was born to sorrow, would yet, even taking survey of their own sad lives, say—life is sweet. That many whose own lives have been bitter enough, think yet that life is sweet, is shown by this, that among them have been found those who have done most to foster the lives of others. But many of them would say that life is sweet, speaking even from their own experience of life. And on the other hand many who are held by those around them to have had little sorrow, who from childhood to old age have scarce ever known pain or suffering, who have had more than their fill of the pleasures of life, and have escaped the usual share of life's afflictions, would speak of life as dull and dreary if not bitter. It has been indeed from such men that the doubting cry has come, Is life worth living? Men of more varied experience would give other answers to that vain question. All answers, indeed must be as idle as the question itself. Yet most men would give the answer which says most for the pleasantness of life—that, as a whole, life is neither bitter nor sweet, neither sharp nor cloying, but that it "has all the charm in bitter-sweetness found."

We are not concerned, however, to inquire what is the true answer to the question, Is life worth living? Though it is clear that if life is not worth living the observed action of evolution has been unfortunate, and the resulting laws of conduct are a mistake, while the reverse must be held if on the whole life is well worth living, yet, so far as our subject of inquiry is concerned, it matters not which view we take. That which is common to both views is all we have to consider. The man who holds that life is worth living, so thinks because he believes that the pleasures of life on the whole outweigh its pains and sorrows. The man who holds that life is not worth living does so because he thinks that the pains and sorrows of life outweigh its pleasures. So much is true independently of all ideas as to what are the real pleasures or the real pains of life, or whether life here is most to be considered or chiefly a future life with pleasures or pains far greater in intensity and in duration than any known here.

"Where or what the chief pleasures or pains of life may be, when or how long endured, in no sort affects the conclusion that life is to be considered worth living or the reverse according as happiness outvies misery or misery happiness, and that therefore the Tightness or wrongness of conduct must be judged not by its direct action on life and the fullness of life but by its indirect influence in increasing or diminishing the totality of happiness. To quote again the words of the great teacher who is so often misquoted and so much misunderstood:

"There is no escape from the admission that in calling good the conduct which subserves life, and bad the conduct which hinders or destroys it, and in so implying that life is a blessing and not a curse, we are inevitably asserting that conduct is good or bad according as its *total* effects are pleasurable or painful." — *Knowledge.*

III

There is only one way of escape from the conclusion reached in our last—that conduct is good or bad according as its total effects are pleasurable or painful—in which statement be it understood the word total *means* total, and is not limited in its application to the person whose conduct is spoken of. If it is supposed that men were created to suffer, that a power which they were bound to obey had planned such suffering, so that any attempt either to take pleasure or to avoid pain was an offense, then of course the conclusion indicated is an erroneous one.

No system of religion has ever definitely taught so hideous a doctrine. Even where sorrow and suffering are recognized as the lot of man, and even where self-inflicted anguish and misery are enjoined as suitable ways of pleasing Deity, it is never said that such sufferings are the ultimate desire of the Supreme Power. These tribulations are all intended for our good: we are to torture ourselves here and now, that hereafter we may avoid much greater pains or enjoy much greater pleasures than here and now we could possibly experience.

Yet underlying this doctrine of greater and longer-lasting happiness as the result of temporary suffering or privation, there has been and is in many so-called religions the doctrine that pain and suffering are pleasing to the gods of inferior creeds and even to the Supreme Power of higher beliefs. The offerings made systematically by some races to their deities imply obviously the belief that the gods are pleased when men deprive themselves of something more or less valued. Sacrifices involving slaughter, whether of domestic animals or of human beings, mean more, for they imply that suffering and death are essentially pleasing to Deity. Even when such gross ideas are removed and religion has been purified, the symbolization of sacrifice in most cases takes the place of sacrifice itself. The conception may and often does remain as an actually vital part of religious doctrine that pleasure is offensive to the Supreme Power and pain pleasing.

If this conception is really recognized, and any men definitely hold that to enjoy or to give pleasure is sinful, because displeasing to God, while the suffering or infliction of pain is commendable, then for them—but for them only—the doctrine is not established that conduct is good or bad according as its total effects are pleasurable or painful. But if there are such men, then they are mentally and morally the direct descendants of the savage of most brutal type, who, because he himself delights to inflict pain, deems his gods to be of kindred nature and immolates victims to them (or, if necessary to gain his ends, shows the reality of his belief by self-torture) to obtain their assistance against his enemies.

If there are such men among us still, then, as Mr. Herbert Spencer says, "we can only recognize the fact that devil-worshipers are not yet extinct." The generality of our conclusions is no more affected by such exceptions as these than it is by the ideas which prevail in Bedlam or Earlswood.

But on the one hand the doctrine thus reached may be passed over as a truism (which it ought to be and indeed is, though, like many truisms, unrecognized); and on the other it may be scouted as Epicurean (which is unmeaning nonsense, however) and as mere pig-philosophy. For it sets happiness as the aim of conduct, and, whether self-happiness or the happiness of others is in question, many find in the mere idea of pleasure as a motive for conduct something unworthy—thereby unconsciously adopting the religious doctrine which has been justly compared with devil-worship.

This expression — Pig-philosophy — has indeed been applied to the doctrine we are considering, by a philosopher who, with Mr. Ruskin and Mr. Matthew Arnold, may be regarded as chief among the wonders of our age—and standing proof of the charm which the British race finds in Constant Grunt, Continual Growl, and Chronic Groan. It must be considered, therefore, as certain that to some minds a philosophy which sets the happiness of self and others as a worthy end must appear unworthy. Such minds find something pig-like in the desire to see the happiness of the world increased. Yet grunting and groaning are at least as characteristic of the porcine race as any desire to increase the comfort of their fellow-creatures or even their own. Mr. Herbert Spencer's lightsome pleasure-doctrine, the essence of which is that we should strive to diminish pain and sorrow (our own included) and to increase joy and happiness, is less suggestive of porcine ways (at least to those who have noted what such ways are) than for instance the following cheerful address to Man: "Despicable biped! what is the sum total of the worst that lies before thee? Death? Well, Death; and say the pangs of Tophet, too, and all that the Devil and Man may, will, or can do against thee! Hast thou not a heart; canst thou not suffer whatsoever it be; and, as a Child of Freedom, though outcast, trample Tophet itself under thy feet, while it consumes thee? "Were this but stern resolution to endure patiently, and even cheerfully, such sorrows as befall man, it were well. Nay, it would fall in with the philosophy of happiness, which enjoins that for their own sake as for the sake of those around them men should bear as lightly as they may their burden of inevitable sorrow. But what Carlyle calls the New-birth or Baphometic Fire-baptism is not Patience but Indignation and Defiance. This is the veritable Pig-philosophy : the "Everlasting No" (*das ewige Nein*) is in truth the Everlasting Grunt of dyspeptic disgust, the constant Oh-Goroo-Goroo of a jaundiced soul.

Are the teachings of living professors of the Everlasting Groan school brighter than those of the gloomy Scotsman? Here are some of the latest utterings of the chief among them: "Loss of life!" exclaims Mr. Ruskin, cheerfully. "By the ship overwhelmed in the river, shattered on the sea; by the mine's blast, the earthquake's burial you mourn for the multitude slain. You cheer the life-boat's crew; you hear with praise and joy the rescue of one still breathing body more at the pit's mouth; and all the while, for one soul that is saved from the momentary passing away (according to your creed, to be with its God), the lost souls yet locked in their polluted flesh haunt, with worse than ghosts, the shadows of your churches and the corners of your streets; and your weary children watch, with no memory of Jerusalem, and no hope of return from *their* captivity, the weltering to the sea of your Waters of Babylon." *Oh! Goroo! Goroo-oo!*

Any philosophy which hopes for other than misery and disgust in life must indeed seem strange doctrine to teachers such as these— even as the smiles of the cheerful seem unmeaning and offensive to those whose souls are overcast with gloom and discontent. Sir Walter Scott tells a story of his childhood which well illustrates the unreasoning hatred felt by the Everlasting Growl school for the doctrine that conduct should be directed to the increase of happiness. One day, his healthy young appetite made him enjoy very heartily the brose or porridge of the family breakfast. Unluckily, he was tempted to say aloud how good he found his food. His father at once ordered a pint of cold water to be thrown in, to spoil the taste of it! Possibly he meant to inculcate what he regarded as a high moral habit; but rather more probably Mr. Walter Scott, Sen., objected to his son's enjoying what he had no taste for himself. Much of the sourness of the Growl Philosophy may be thus interpreted.

Chap.3
Self *Versus* Others

I

We teach our children, the preacher tells his flock, but few follow the precept—Care more for others than for self. It sounds a harsh doctrine to say, instead—Each must care for himself before others. Yet it is not only true teaching, it is a self-evident truth. It would not be even worth saying, so obviously true is it, were it not that in putting aside the doctrine because of its seeming harshness men over- look, or try to overlook, the important consequences which follow from it.

If a man's whole soul—nay, let me speak for a moment in my proper person—if my whole soul were filled with the thought that my one chief business in life is to make those around me, as far as I can make my influence felt, as happy as possible, to increase in every possible way the stock of human (nay, also of animal) happiness, I must still begin by taking care of myself. For if, through want of care, I myself should cease to exist, I can no longer, in any way, serve others; nay, it is even conceivable that my immature disappearance from the scene of my proposed exertions for others' benefit might cause some diminution of the totality of happiness.

If the very thought of care for self should suggest that there can be no real love or care for others where self-care comes first (self-evident though the proposition be that care of self *must* come first), let us replace the case rejected as imaginary by a concrete and familiar illustration.

None can question the unselfishness of the love which a mother feels for her infant babe. None can doubt that, if question arose between the babe's life and hers, her own life would be willingly sacrificed. Of course there are exceptions, perhaps many, but no one can doubt, and multitudes of cases have proved, that the rule holds generally. Now, the nursing mother not only has, in her very love for her babe, to take care of herself, but to care for herself *first*, and to take more care of herself than, but for her pure, unselfish love for her child, she would have troubled herself to take.

Let this case suffice to show that care of self before others (not, therefore, necessarily more than others), besides being a self-evident duty (which many may regard as a mere trifle), may be not only perfectly consistent with regard for others, and even with devotion to others, but may be absolutely essential to the proper discharge of our duties toward others. In fact, it is little more than a truism, instead of being, as many would at a first view imagine, a paradox, that the more earnest our wish to increase the happiness of others, the more carefully must we look after our own welfare.

If we take a wider view, and, instead of considering a single life, study the development of families and races, we still find the same lesson. As the man who wishes his life to be useful to his fellows and to increase their happiness must take care of that life, so he who would wish to benefit humanity through his family or race must not only nourish his own life and strength, but must develop those activities which advance his own welfare and the welfare of his family. Otherwise come, inevitably, the dwindling of the faculties on which his own value depends, and the loss in his descendants of good qualities which they might otherwise have inherited from him. Or it may be that such qualities are inherited in less degree than had he duly exercised powers and capacities which were in a sense held in trust for them. "We are apt to overlook the importance of individual action in such cases, not noticing that the progress of a race depends on the aggregate of acts by the individual members of the race.

To take a concrete instance here, as of the simpler case: If a number of persons in any nation or at any epoch, impelled by a desire to benefit their fellows, devote their lives to celibacy, they influence in important degree the qualities of the next and succeeding generations. They diminish the proportion in which their personal qualities—presumably valuable—will appear in future generations, and relatively increase the proportion of other and less desirable qualities. This is obvious enough. It should, however, be almost as clear that, in whatever degree such persons in a community as possess the best qualities fail to advance, in all things just, their personal interests, they diminish the influence of the better qualities, not only in their own time, but in times to come. If, to take another concrete example, all persons of the better sort, forgetting their duties to themselves and their race, enter of set purpose on lives of poverty, asceticism, and dreariness, they not only diminish in large degree the good they might do during life, but they injure their offspring, and, through them, posterity.

Under its biological aspect, then, the doctrine that care of self must necessarily take precedence of care and thought for others, is incontestable—it is the merest truism—though many speak, and some act, as if the doctrine were iniquitous. But this doctrine has its moral aspect also. The question of duty comes in at once and very obviously so soon as the actual consequences of conduct have been shown to be good or bad. But it may be well to show more definitely what the true line of duty is in regard to self. I shall, therefore, next consider cases where self-abnegation leads directly to the diminution of general happiness.—*Knowledge.*

II

A man's power of increasing happiness depends both directly and indirectly on his fitness for the occupations of his life. Directly, because if unfit, whether through ill health or inaptitude, he works with pain instead of pleasure, and because he gives less satisfaction or causes actual annoyance to those for whom his occupations, whatsoever they may be, are pursued. Indirectly, because as a result of work pursued under such conditions he suffers in temper and quality as a member of the body social. Hence all such care of self as is shown by attention to bodily health, by the careful culture of personal good qualities, by just apportionment of time to personal requirements, and so forth, may be regarded as of the nature of duty. In such degree as pleasure, recreation, change of scene, quiet, and the like, are necessary for the maintenance or improvement of the health, the care to secure these, so far from being held to be a concession to self, should be esteemed a most important point in "the whole duty of man."

A narrow view of duty to others may direct attention to what lies near at hand. Just as the savage consumes, to satisfy the hunger of a day, seed which should have been devoted to provide for many days in the future which lies beyond his ken, so the man who has no thought but of what lies near at hand, is apt to sacrifice health, strength, and fitness for work, from which great and long-lasting benefits might have been reaped, to obtain painfully and uncomfortably much smaller results. By overwork and self-sacrifice—self-devotion if you will—a man may in a few years effect much material good to those around him—perhaps more than in the time he could have effected by a wiser apportionment of his work and strength. But at the end of a much shorter period of work than he could have accomplished with ease and pleasantness, ere a tithe perhaps of the good he was really competent to do has been effected, his health breaks down, his strength fails him, he can no longer do the good he wanted so much to do. Nay, worse, life not only becomes a burden to him, but he becomes a burden to others. A wise and thoughtful care of self would have avoided this. Such care of self, then, even if regarded from the point of view which should be taken by the rest, is simply far-sighted regard for others.

Perhaps the simplest way of testing the matter is by considering what would happen if all or many of the members of a community followed a course which is commonly spoken of as if it were meritorious. It is manifest that a community chiefly composed of persons who neglecting self broke down their health and strength in exhausting efforts to advance the well-being of others would be a community constantly burdened by fresh accessions of worn-out and used-up members—including eventually most of those who had been most anxious to serve their fellows.

But the question becomes still more serious when the known facts of heredity are taken into account. The evil effects of self-neglect, whether in the form of overwork, or asceticism, or avoidance of all such pleasurable emotions as lighten the toils and worries of life, or in other ways, affect posterity as well as the individual life. Ill-health and weakness are transmitted to children and to children's children through many generations. It is not going too far to say that on the average more misery is wrought and to a much greater number by neglect of self than can be matched by any amount of benefit conferred during life, still less by such benefit as directly arises from self-sacrifice. A man shall work day after day beyond his strength for ten years, and by such excess of activity shall perhaps accumulate at the expense of a ruined constitution what may confer a certain amount of happiness on several persons, or keep discomfort from them. Probably with better-advised efforts during that time more real good might have been conferred on those same persons, for man does not live by bread alone; and certainly in the long run even of a single ordinary life much more good may be done by combining zeal for others with due regard for the welfare of self. But when we consider the multiplied misery inherited by the offspring of weak, sickly, and gloomy parents, we see that even though, on the whole, there had been during life a balance in favor of happiness conferred, this—more than out-weighed even in the first generation—would be many hundred times outweighed in the long run.

CARE FOR SELF AS A DUTY.

The thought seems strange to many that in conduct which appears to them mere care of self there may be further-seeing regard for others than in simple self-sacrifice. Yet the matter is so obvious when pointed out as to suggest later a different sort of retort—namely, that it was scarce worth pointing out. Only, as it happens that this truly obvious matter has been grievously overlooked, as the teacher of this essentially true and therefore demonstrable lesson has been rebuked for inculcating mere self-seeking, it is tolerably clear that the lesson was very much needed.

Let us consider how obviously true it is, however, as he presents it. Take, for instance, the matter on which I touched in my last—viz., the consideration of the known laws of heredity. "When we remember," says the clear, calm teacher of our time, "how commonly it is remarked that high health and overflowing spirits render any lot in life tolerable, while chronic ailments make gloomy a life most favorably circumstanced, it becomes amazing that both the world at large and writers who make conduct their study should ignore the terrible evils which disregard of personal well-being inflicts on the unborn, and the incalculable good laid up for the unborn by attention to personal well-being. Of all bequests of parents to children the most valuable is a sound constitution. Though a man's body is not a property that can be inherited, yet his constitution may fitly be compared to an entailed estate; and, if he rightly understands his duty to posterity, he will see that he is bound to pass on that estate uninjured if not improved. To say this is to say that he must be egoistic to the extent of satisfying all those desires associated with the due performance of functions. Nay, it is to say more. It is to say that he must seek in due amounts the various pleasures which life offers. For beyond the effect these have in raising the tide of life and maintaining constitutional vigor, there is the effect they have in preserving and increasing a capacity for receiving enjoyment. Endowed with abundant energies and various tastes, some can get gratifications of many kinds on opportunities hourly occurring; while others are so inert, and so uninterested in things around, that they can not even take the trouble to amuse themselves. And, unless heredity be denied, the inference must be that due acceptance of the miscellaneous pleasures life offers conduces to the capacity for enjoyment in posterity; and that persistence in dull, monotonous life by parents diminishes the ability of their descendants to make the best of what gratifications fall to them."

All this is clear and obvious enough when thus pointed out; though the very passage in which Mr. Spencer here so clearly shows that to be happy, so far as by due regard of personal well-being one can make one's self happy, is a duty, has been selected for abuse as though he taught simply this—seek to gratify self in every available way. The kind of rebuke justly passed on those who in the search for pleasure, in mere self-gratification, ruin their health, lose happiness, become morose, gloomy, and misanthropic, lose taste for all pleasures lower as well as higher, and hand on to their children and their children's children these and other evil effects of the grosser forms of self-indulgence, has been passed upon the teacher of that farseing care of self by which the health is preserved, happiness obtained, the whole nature strengthened and sweetened, the enjoyment of all forms of pleasure increased, and in all these respects the lot of posterity improved to many—nay, to uncounted generations.

On the other hand, there are those who, seeing that the doctrine taught is unassailable on that side, assert that it is and always has been obvious—forgetting how many morose and gloomy people there are who show by their mere existence that in the past (of which they are the descendants) the contrary doctrine has prevailed, as it still exists in the present (which they in part represent), and will continue doubtless for many generations.

If it be agreed that Mr. Spencer's teaching in this matter is needless where it is accepted and useless where it is needed (because none who would be benefited by it will listen), I answer that the case is otherwise. There are thousands now, and their number will be largely increased in the future, who have found in this teaching the lesson which they needed to make their lives happy and their influence in their own time and in the future blessed. It has come as a new and cheering light to them (I was going to say as a revelation, but the word would be misinterpreted) to see in happiness, their own included, the answer to the doleful question. Is life worth living? If by self-mortification, overwork, wear end worry, I make myself wretched and fail to make those around me happier, I may well ask in mournful accents that foolish question. If I not only fail so to make others happier but make them less happy, and hand on gloom and misery to future ages, I may not only ask it gloomily but answer it sadly. Life is not worth living. Better, were it lawful, to cease the painful and useless, the worse than useless, contest. But if by due care and thought of self, by reasonable enjoyment of the bright and pleasant things which life brings to most, I in some degree or wholly counterpoise such pains and sorrows as life brings to all, and at the same time help to brighten the lives of those around, and those also of generations as yet unborn, how shall I doubt what answer to give to the question. Is life worth living? Not sad is the answer, but bright and cheering.

There is still not a little to be said respecting the due care of personal well-being. Just here I close by remarking that, in the attempt to simplify Mr. Herbert Spencer's nomenclature, I certainly did not improve the title of this chapter by calling it "Self *versus* Others" as I did till now, instead of "Egoism *versus* Altruism," as he called the chapter in the "Data of Ethics" bearing on the same subject. Due care of self is not a matter of "self versus others," seeing that care of personal well-being is essential to the influence of self for the good of others. I have therefore given to this section a new sub-title.

But there is another aspect of this part of our subject which requires careful attention. We have already touched on the effects which would follow if all the members of society in their zeal for the interest of others disregarded the requirements of their own health and well-being, and overlooked the effects of unwise neglect of self on the interests of their descendants, and therefore of the society of which their descendants would form part. Nor, in considering this aspect of the subject, have we been dealing with imaginary evils, seeing that many of the defects of the body social at the present day can be clearly traced to such misdirected, though well-meaning, efforts on the part of the better sort in past ages.

But, when we consider the mixed nature of all communities, the mischief of ill-regulated disinterestedness as compared with far-seeing consideration of the interests of family, race, and nation, becomes more obviously a matter of practical moment.

If *all* men sought the good of others before their own, it is obvious that a confusion of interests would arise — other but not less unsatisfactory, perhaps, than that which exists in a society where, let their doctrines be what they may, the greater number seek their own welfare first. If, on the other hand, *all* men were moved by far-seeing considerations and a well-regulated care for the interests of others, no special care would be needed, and few rules would have to be laid down, to insure the progress and happiness of the community. But, as a matter of fact, neither one nor the other state of things exists. The body social as at present existing may be classified, as regards care for others and self-seeking, into the following principal divisions:

A). First, there are those who in precept, and as far as they can in practice also, think of others before themselves, who repay injuries by benefits, answer reviling by blessing, and adopt as their rule the principle that those who injure and hate them are those whom they should chiefly love and toward whose well-being their efforts should be chiefly directed. This class is very small; it is always losing members, but is probably increased by fresh accessions about as fast as it is diminished by those who leave it.

B). Secondly, there are those who, having for their chief aim the well-being of those around them and of mankind generally, yet recognize as necessary even for the advancement of that object, a due regard for the well-being—the health, strength, cheerfulness, and even the material prosperity—of self. This class, like the first, is small; but steadily increases in every advancing community.

C). Thirdly, come those who in all societies, at present, form far the greater part of the community —those, *viz.*, who think chiefly of their own interests or their families', yet, though not specially careful to increase the happiness of others, are not selfishly intent on their own well-being only.

D). Fourthly, there are those who think solely of themselves, or, if they look beyond themselves, care only for their nearest kinsfolk, consciously disregarding the interests of others, and seeking only in the struggle for life the advancement of themselves or their families.

E). Lastly, there are those who, in their struggle to advance self, are prepared to prey on others if need be; in other words, willfully to do mischief to others for their own advantage.

In this classification we consider only the actual conduct of the various orders, not their expressed opinions. Were these to be taken into account, the classification would remain nominally unchanged, but the numbers belonging to the different classes would be very much altered. Most of the members of the body social in civilized, and especially in Christian countries, would be assigned in that case to Class A — though everyone knows that in reality this class is a very small one indeed. Class B would be scarcely changed in number, because, while members of that class are ready to maintain that the views on which their conduct depends are, in their opinion, sound and just, these views are not such as the members of other classes are anxious to simulate. They are not popular views, like the self-sacrificing ones which so many pretend to hold, but by no means really act upon.

It is tolerably obvious that the well-being of society as a whole requires that Classes D and E shall not be unduly large, compared with the whole number of the community. Whatever tends to diminish their number, and especially the number of Class E, must tend to increase the well-being — that is, the happiness — of the social body. Class C, which always constitutes the main body, merges by insensible gradations into Class D, and Class D into Class E. Comparatively slight changes, influences relatively unimportant, suffice to transfer large numbers from the indifferent Class C to the self-seeking Class D, and similarly slight changes may suffice to transfer many from the simply self-seeking Class D to the noxious Class E. The lines of distinction between the first three classes are more marked. Members of the first class are more apt, at present, to pass into the third class than into the second, though little it should seem is needed to make these (the self-forgetting, enemy-loving members of the community) pass into the section combining due care of self with anxious desire to increase the happiness and well-being of the social body. That any members of the second class should pass either into the first, whence most of them came, or into the third, whose indifference to the welfare of others is unpleasing to them, or into the fourth, whose selfishness is abhorrent to them, is unlikely; for which reason this class should logically have occupied the first place, seeing that the class we have set first really merges both into the second and into the third, which should, therefore, be set on different sides of it. We had a reason, however, which many will understand, for not depriving Class A of the position it holds theoretically, though practically the class has no such standing, and is especially contemned by Class C, the noisiest in pretending to accept its principles.

Since, then, the welfare of the body social depends mainly on the relative smallness of Classes D and E, the selfish and the noxious, it follows that an important, if not the chief, duty to society, for all who really and reasoningly desire the well-being and progress of the community, is so to regulate their conduct as to cause these classes to become relatively smaller and smaller. Conduct which can be shown to encourage the development of these classes, to make selfish ways pleasanter, and noxious ways safer, is injurious to the body social, and is therefore *wrong;* while, on the contrary, conduct which tends to increase relatively the number of those who are considerate of the welfare of others, is beneficial to the community, tends to increase the happiness of the greater number, and is therefore right. If, therefore, it can be shown that the principle adopted by Class A, however self-sacrificing, must tend to work far wider mischief in encouraging the development of selfishness and wrong-doing than it can possibly effect in the way of good (the good being local and casual, the evil systematic and wide-spread), then will it become clear that the principle adopted by Class B, which equally seeks the good of others, but entirely avoids the risk of encouraging the selfish and the evil-disposed, is that which can alone lead to permanent improvement and happiness in the social body.

This, as we shall next proceed to show, is unquestionably the case.— *Knowledge.*

III

It will perhaps be sufficient, in response to numerous inquiries addressed to me respecting the supposed religious bearing of these papers, to remark that they are not intended to have any religious bearing whatsoever. I am simply inquiring what are the rules of conduct suggested when each person takes as his guiding principle the increase of the happiness of those around, an expression which must be taken as including himself in the same somewhat Hibernian sense in which Milton included Adam among "those since born, his sons." I may add that nearly all the letters addressed to me have been interesting, and some have been singularly well-reasoned—all utterly unlike the rather spiteful and very silly letters I referred to in a foot-note to my last paper. Yet I cannot suffer the religious element to be imported into the subject— no matter how courteously or kindly the thing may be done. I have just the same objection to see the question of the evolution of conduct considered from that side, which the student of astronomy or geology has against dealing with the objections and difficulties raised by those who seem always to suspect that under the teachings of God's work, the universe, there may lie some grievous deceptions if not some monstrous falsehoods. If my reasoning is bad, it can be met and overcome on its own ground.

I may, however, make this general remark with regard to all systems of morality whatsoever, including those which have come before men in company with religious teachings. Without a single exception every one of these systems includes—and professes to include—features suitable to the special time and the special place when and where it was propounded. How much of any system may thus be regarded as local or temporary or both may be a moot point; but that some of each system is of that sort is absolutely certain. "Because of the hardness" of men's hearts the Mosaic system, for instance, had certain rules; and, because of the weakness of their hearts (who can doubt it?), the system which replaced that of Moses had certain other rules. The same is true of every system of conduct ever propounded. We may believe the rule sound and good in its own time and place, "Whosoever shall smite you on the right cheek turn to him the other also," and "If any man will sue thee at the law and take away thy coat, let him have thy cloak also." A man may believe these rules to be more than sound and good, to be of divine origin— yet recognize that in our own time, and here, in Europe or America, the rules would work ill. He who so taught recognized in the same way that other rules which had been good in their time had lost their virtue with changing manners. He knew *where* it is written, "Thou shalt give life for life, eye for eye, tooth for tooth," and so on; yet he only quoted these Scripture teachings to correct them—"But *I* say unto you, that ye resist not evil, but whosoever," etc. When he thus corrected what was "said by them of old time," he did not show disrespect—whatever the Scribes and Pharisees tried to make out—for the teachers of old time, whose words he read and expounded. He knew that "old times were changed," and therefore old manners and morals gone. He said, "Suffer little children to come unto me," and loved them, *not* teaching—as had seemed more convenient and was (let us believe) better, in earlier days—that the child would be spoiled unless diligently belabored with the rod.

These times and the races and the nations now most prominent on the earth are even more unlike the community in Palestine nineteen centuries ago, than that community was unlike the Jewish people in the days of the more ancient lawgiver. The opponents of evolution may prefer to believe that the human race has been stereotyped; but facts are a little against them. And even if we admitted the imagined fixedness of the human race for nineteen centuries, they would still have to explain the contradiction between two systems for both of which they find the same authority. Of course, there is no real or at least no necessary contradiction. Grant the human race to be what we know it to be, a constantly developing family, and the contradiction vanishes—we simply learn that what is best for one time is not best for another, even among one and the same people; how much more, then, must the best rules of conduct vary when different peoples as well as different times are considered!

All this, however, is a disgression, which should have been unnecessary, but has in a sense been forced on me by the misapprehensions of many well-meaning critics (and a few who are not well-meaning at all, but of the Honeythunder order, teaching the law of love by reviling and worse).

The duty which each man owes to himself in regard to the maintenance of his health, the development of his powers, and so forth, which becomes a duty to others when regarded with reference to those more immediately around him or dependent upon him, and is still manifestly a duty in relation to others where the advancement of the general well-being, so far as he can influence it, is considered, has another aspect when considered in reference to those classes (D and E) whose encouragement or increase would be injurious to the body social. It is not only essential to the evolution of conduct in the right direction that those who may be classed as "men of good will" should increase relatively in number and influence, but also that those who are either absolutely men of ill-will, or are so far not of good-will that they disregard the well-being of others, should be checked and discouraged.

This requirement for the evolution of the more altruistic kind of conduct involves in many cases—as a duty—conduct of a kind which the few real members of Class A and the many members of Class C who speak of themselves as belonging to Class A—regard as self-assertive. It becomes a duty, when the matter is viewed in this light, to assert just rights and resist wrongful claims. For, every act of carelessness or self-neglect in such matters tends to the encouragement of the less valuable or noxious classes which profit by it. It may be that to uphold just claims or resist wrong-doing may be less comfortable than to give way. In such a case the duty becomes an altruistic one, however egoistic the action based on the consideration of such duty may appear. But in a number of cases the claim upheld may be well worth upholding in itself, the wrong resisted may involve gross injury. In such a case the care of a personal right or the resistance of a wrong is, in itself, egoistic. Yet may it well be that the person concerned may esteem it better to give up the claim or to yield to the wrong, until he recognizes that the idea of self-sacrifice, however beautiful in itself, may involve a far-reaching wrong to the better members of the body social.

We touch here on considerations which are in question every day, almost every hour, of our lives.

Consider home-life, for example. In nearly every home there are those who are disposed to take unfair advantage of the rest; and they are far better restrained by the quiet resistance of their attempts than in any other way—certainly far better than by yielding, continued till nothing but the anger roused by some attempt, more barefaced than the rest, moves to resistance. We see this especially exemplified in the families of careless parents—unselfish perhaps in a sense, but really negligent of their duties. It has been said for this reason that unselfish parents have commonly selfish children, which seems contrary to the law of heredity, but illustrates rather the natural influence of defective training. The fact really is, that the children of selfish parents are as a rule more selfish in character than those of the unselfish; they grow up to be as unpleasant in their ways as the children of careless, unwatchful parents; and their unpleasantness is more apt to be permanent. Yet the unchecked ways of children whose parents yield unwisely to them, illustrate well on a small scale (even though happily the mischief is often transient) how the assertion of just claims, and the restraint of wrong-doing, involve a form of egoism which must be regarded as a duty.

In life outside the family, we constantly find the duty of resisting evil presenting itself in apparently egoistic aspect. In hundreds of ways the members of Class C show their readiness to become members of Class D and members of class D to develop their unpleasant ways. The adoption of considerate habits and care for the just claims of others in all the multitudinous details of our daily life, constantly lead to attempts by the selfish and obnoxious to take advantage of what they regard as mere weakness of disposition. In such cases, while it is by no means desirable to give up ways which are in themselves essential to the well-being of the society of which we form part, we must—as a duty—resist the encroachments of objectionable persons—not the less that the matter insisted upon is one to which we attach importance, so that our firmness has its egoistic aspect. Men are but children of a larger growth, and there is no surer or better way of eliminating at least the grosser forms of selfishness than by so resisting unjust claims that they—simply fail. This is the appropriate punishment—akin to that which Mr. Spencer regards (most justly in my opinion) as the only proper form of punishment for children, viz., punishment which is the direct consequence of ill conduct. Of course, it will happen that mere resistance of a wrong may bring definite punishment—directly or indirectly—to the wrong-doer; but (apart from such cases, in which we have to ask whether justice may not need to be tempered with mercy) all I would insist on is that the selfish, grasping, oppressive members of the body social should be so resisted that, whenever it is possible, they fail of their unfair purpose.

The rule applies in small matters as well as great. Mr. Spencer himself notes (though it is when dealing with selfishness specifically) a case of not infrequent occurrence, and perhaps of a trifling enough kind—the acted falsehood of railway-passengers who, by dispersed coats, make a traveler believe that all the seats in a compartment are taken when they are not. Here the detection and resistance of an attempted wrong, contemptible as it is, may excite some sense of shame in the wrong-doers, though conceivably not (for such wrongdoers are of a shameless sort); but the defeat of their purpose will at the least involve disappointment and serve as a discouragement from such attempts in the future. Of course, a very zealous opponent of the obnoxious section of society might not be content with what I here advocate as the simple line of duty in such cases. He might (as an earnest opponent of evil did—rather harshly I think—the other day) take on himself to punish as well as to resist evil; and having been met with the customary falsehood as to some article deposited in a vacant seat, might pitch it out of the window, with the remark that he would be responsible to the real owner when he appeared. But this is going beyond the strict line of duty in such matters.

It will appear manifest, I think, on careful consideration of the matter by anyone who notes, for a few days or even hours, the course of events around him in his family and in society, that he who neglects to defend his own rights against the encroachments of Class D as well as of Class E, and of Class C as well as of Class D, fails as clearly in his duty to the social body as the parent who overlooks selfish and unruly conduct in his children. And just as the children themselves whose training is thus neglected have really just reason, did they but know what is good for them, to complain of such mistaken kindness, so even the more selfish (all but the members of Class E) have no less reason than the unselfish, did they but know their own interests, to desire that considerate but firm and self-regardful conduct should prevail throughout the body social.

It has been shown that care of self necessarily precedes care of others, because we must ourselves live if we are to benefit others. It has been shown further that if there is to be progress and improvement in the race, the superior must profit by their superiority, and so develop in numbers and influence, while the inferior because inferior become less and less predominant in the community. Further, it has appeared that while a society improves as it becomes constituted more and more largely of the better sort, this improvement depends in large part on those qualities of the individual members of society which depend on due care of self. In like manner it appears that in a society whose members are not duly regardful of self, misery arises from the excess of self-denial which ends by making those who practice it burdens on the rest of the community. Lastly, we have seen that due care of self is desirable, and neglect of the just rights of self injurious to the social body, because that undue care of self which is properly called selfishness, and leads either to negative or positive forms of wrong-doing, thrives and multiplies in a community where the better sort allow evil and oppression to pass unchecked by the due assertion of self-rights.

But now it is worth remarking that the line of reasoning which has been followed does not in reality indicate changed conduct. It reconciles the actual conduct of the better sorts of men with rules derived from observed facts and laws in regard to the development of conduct, and would tend to reconcile their conduct with their words, if men in general would but recognize the folly and danger of a system by which they have one set of rules on their lips and another for their actual guidance. As Mr. Herbert Spencer well puts it, the general conclusion to which we have been led, "though at variance with nominally accepted beliefs, is not at variance with actually accepted beliefs; while opposed to the doctrine which men are taught should be acted upon, it is in harmony with the doctrine which they do act upon and dimly see must be acted upon.... The laborer looking for wages in return for work done, no less than the merchant who sells goods at a profit, the doctor who expects fees for advice, or the priest who calls the scene of his ministrations a 'living,' assumes as beyond question the truth that selfishness, carried to the extent of enforcing his claims and enjoying the returns his efforts bring, is not only legitimate but essential. Even persons who avow a contrary conviction prove by their acts that it is inoperative. Those who repeat with emphasis the maxim, 'Love your neighbor as yourself,' do not render up what they possess so as to satisfy the desires of all as much as they satisfy their own desires. Nor do those whose extreme maxim is, 'Live for others,' differ appreciably from people around in their regards for personal welfare, or fail to appropriate their shares of life's pleasures. In short, that which is set forth above as the belief to which scientific ethics lead us, is that which men do really believe, as distinguished from that which they believe they believe—or pretend they believe."

Which is better?—to proclaim with our lips rules of conduct which none of us really follow, and to denounce those who show that the rules which the best-minded among us really strive to follow are such as tend most to improve the condition of the body social, or frankly to recognize the just and equitable rules of conduct which after all are the real guides of the actions of all well-meaning men? Is it well or wise to discredit these fair and proper rules by setting up others which seem more self-sacrificing, but which none except a few abnormally-minded persons of no influence (objects of ill-concealed contempt among those who applaud such rules) actually strive to follow— rules, moreover, which if widely followed would inevitably bring misery on the community? For my own part I believe that the system by which rules no sane man follows are set up as the real laws of conduct, works most serious mischief, by discouraging many from the attempt to be consistently fair and just to those around them as well as to themselves. Of what use, they feel (rather than consciously think), is any attempt to be merely just and considerate, when still we fall far short of the standard set up for our guidance? Apart from this lies the direct mischief to character which necessarily arises from the confident expression of acceptance of rules which every man (except the few abnormal creatures I have mentioned) knows well that he does not follow, has never attempted to follow, and never intends to follow. Many are led, through their honest unwillingness thus to falsify their words by their actions, into an error of the opposite kind; preferring rather to maintain rules of conduct which have a selfish aspect, while their actual conduct is unselfish, than to ape a degree of disinterestedness which they do not possess, and which would (they know) be mischievous if really possessed and acted upon by any large proportion of the community.

But, lastly, let it be noticed that just care for self does not imply necessarily less care for others, but often more. As a mere matter of fact, men who carefully consider their own just claims are found to be more considerate, as a rule, of the claims of others, than those who assert that men ought not to be careful to consider what their just claims are.

Horace long since, in his famous ode beginning *"Justum ac tenacem propositi virum,"* drew attention to the connection commonly existing between justice and firm maintenance of what is due to self. Of course, there are men who are unduly regardful of self, not being content with the maintenance of their own rights, but willfully infringing the rights of others. Equally are there some who while negligent of their own rights are considerate of those of others. But these are the exceptions. As a rule one may recognize in due regard for self-rights the same principle which displays itself otherwise in care for the rights of others. Considering social as distinguished from individual opinions, assuredly Mr. Spencer is justified in what he says on the egoistic excesses which often accompany excessive altruism: "A society in which the most exalted principles of self-sacrifice for the benefit of neighbors are enunciated, may be a society in which unscrupulous sacrifice of alien fellow-creatures is not only tolerated but applauded. Along with professed anxiety to spread these exalted opinions among heathens, there may go the deliberate fastening of a quarrel upon them with a view to annexing their territory. Men who every Sunday have listened aprovingly to injunctions carrying the regard for other men to an impracticable extent, may yet hire themselves out to slay, at the word of command, any people in any part of the world, utterly indifferent to the right or wrong of the matter fought about. And as in these cases transcendent altruism in theory co-exists with brutal egoism in practice, so conversely a more qualified altruism may have for its concomitant a greatly moderated egoism. For, asserting the due claims of self is, by implication, drawing a limit beyond which the claims are undue; and is, by consequence, bringing into greater clearness the claims of others."

We have next to consider the duty of caring for others, as it presents itself in connection with the morality of happiness.—*Knowledge.*

CARE OF OTHERS AS A DUTY.

I enter now on a portion of my subject where I shall seem less at issue with those who repeat with their lips, and fancy they hold in their hearts (though they never think of following in their lives), certain rules of conduct in which due care of self is treated as objectionable and evil is spoken of as not to be resisted but encouraged. I shall still be at issue with those who assert, apparently without thinking—certainly without alleging any reasons—

that conduct and duty are not matters for scientific discussion at all, that they have no scientific aspect, and that such considerations as the progress and improvement of life, the increase of the fullness and happiness of life, and so forth, have no bearing whatever, and should have none, on our opinion as to what is right or wrong. But we may very well afford to disregard objections having so little relation to actual facts. Every one really guides his conduct in large part by such considerations as many thus allege to have no proper bearing on conduct; nor can anyone draw a line beyond which such considerations must not operate: when any one has tried to do so, and perhaps imagines he has succeeded, then I shall simply meet his objection with the remark that he need consider what I have said and what I may hereafter say as only applying to such parts of conduct as he has admitted to be within the range of scientific discussion.

Let us take, now, the doctrine that while due care of self comes to each man, and indeed to every creature having life, as essentially *first*, yet due care of others—though second to due care of self—is as absolutely essential. The two are interdependent—and that to such degree that neither can exist without the other. The great difference in the treatment which science has to extend to the two forms of duty—the egoistic and the altruistic—

resides in this, that whereas in insisting on egoistic duties science is really insisting on what every normally-constituted man is already apt to attend to, in insisting on altruistic duties science is insisting on duties woefully neglected, despite the fervor with which they are verbally enjoined. Many reject egoistic duties in words, who look so carefully after their own interests in action that those who inculcate due care of self as a duty are ashamed to have to admit such utter selfishness as among the results (the wholesome fruits, as it were) of the process of development which conduct, like all things else, has undergone, is undergoing, and will ever continue to undergo. The truth is, that the careful study of what may be rightly sought and claimed for self is no unworthy preparation for due thought and care of others.

Let us briefly trace the development of altruism.

In many of the lower forms of animal life, the acts which tend to race-maintenance are altruistic. The parent is sacrificed wholly or partially in the production of progeny. Nor even in the higher forms of life does this form of sacrifice disappear, though the very beginning of new existences may involve egoistic rather than altruistic relations. Unconsciously at first, but consciously afterward, and later still by definite actions to that end directed, the mother of each new member of even the human race divine sacrifices herself for her offspring. We may be said to imbibe altruism with our mothers' milk. Every act by which in babyhood our life was fostered was a practical exemplification of the doctrine that care of others is essential to the maintenance and progress of the race. To altruism each one of us owes life itself, and the human race owes its existence as certainly to altruism, though such altruism was secondary to egoism in its influence.

And note here, in passing, how development of conduct is related to this early altruistic care of the individual life. As certainly as a want of due care of self leads to the diminution of altruism, by causing those who are not duly egoistic to disappear from the scene of life and leave no successors or few, so does want of due care of others, in the nourishment and rearing of offspring, lead inevitably to the diminution and eventual disappearance of types not sufficiently altruistic. The careless, unloving mother is unconsciously doing her part in eliminating selfishness from the world (the process, however slow, is a sure one), for the child she neglects shares her nature, and must thrive less than a child of happier nature nursed and cared for by a more loving mother. In whatever degree individual instances may seem to tell against this process of evolution, in the average of many cases and through many generations the law must certainly tell.

Nor is this law limited to the influence of the parent who has most to do with the earlier years of life. Throughout childhood and in greater or less degree to the hour and even beyond the hour when each man and each woman begins to take part in the duties of life, and in most cases in the actual struggle for life, development depends on cares which will be well bestowed by unselfish parents, and so tend to increase the amount and fullness of unselfish life, while the selfish will neglect them, and so unconsciously help to eliminate (in the long run) the more selfish natures. It must be so if there is any truth in the doctrine of heredity, and the doctrine is not only true but is universally recognized: it is scarcely more clearly and certainly recognized now than it was by those who in old times made the pregnant proverb, full of old-world wisdom and experience, "The fathers have eaten sour grapes, and the children's teeth are set on edge." Fathers and mothers who are selfish by nature rear with less care offspring who as certainly inherit their nature as the young of beasts of prey inherit the carnivorous tastes of those to whom they owe their lives. Hence, fortunately for the race—seeing how many egoistic tendencies are apt to be fostered in the struggle for life—a constant tendency to the elimination of the more selfish natures.

To this may be added the consideration that the ill-reared and unduly egoistic are less likely than those of more generous and altruistic nature to be found pleasing by those of the opposite sex, less likely therefore to marry, so that (speaking always of the average not of individual cases) there is yet another factor opposing the increase in number of the unduly egoistic.

Thus do we recognize on the one hand that within families a due degree of altruism is essential to the development of life and life's fullness, while on the other hand undue egoism tends directly in more ways than one to diminish happiness.

The best proof that such influence is exerted is found in the circumstance that in every advancing community the young are cared for with constantly-increasing care. Among savage races offspring receive few altruistic attentions. They are not reared in the full sense of the word. Almost from the beginning of their lives they have to take part in the struggle for life. In civilized communities they are cared for during many years, and they are better, more thoroughly, and more wisely, cared for, the more such communities advance. All this indicates and enables us to measure the development of altruism, so far as the family is concerned.

And that care of others in this case (i.e., within the family) is not only essential to the development of life and its fullness, but also to the happiness of self, will be clear if we consider the matter with the least attention. For the altruistic nature shown in the care of children is inherited by children and developed in them by such care. Hence, as Mr. Spencer well notes, there results such conduct on the part of children as "makes parenthood a blessing." Of the parent of children inheriting such natures and so reared, it may be said that, even in our days (to which the saying of the Hebrew Psalmist was not, I suppose, intended originally to apply), the man is blessed that hath his quiver full of them. On the contrary, where the parents and therefore probably the children are of selfish nature, and the example set the children is unduly egoistic, parenthood is no blessing, and may well become a source of misery. What happens in this case? asks the philosopher whose treatment of the scientific aspect of duty we are following. "First the domestic irritations must be relatively great; for the actions of selfish children to one another and to their parents cause daily aggressions and squabbles. Second, when adult, such children are more likely than others to dissatisfy employers, alienate friends, and compromise the family by misbehavior, or even by crime. Third, beyond the sorrows thus brought on them, the parents of such children have eventually to bear the sorrows of neglected old age. The cruelty shown in extreme degrees by savages who leave the decrepit to starve is shown in a measure by all unsympathetic sons and daughters to their unsympathetic fathers and mothers; and these, in their latter days, suffer from transmitted callousness in proportion as they have been callous in the treatment of those around. Browning's versified story 'Halbert and Hob' typifies this truth."

We turn next from altruism in the family to altruism as an essential part of social conduct.

The relations within a family present on a small scale a picture of the relations among the members of a race or nation, as these in turn present a miniature of the relations between the different races and nations which form the human family. As men rise in the scale of being, they pass from the sense of duty within the family to the sense of duty between man and man throughout society, and thence—though as yet this development is very limited—to the sense of right between different races and nations. We have seen that undue care of self is self-injurious and eventually must be self-destructive in the family. There is a corresponding law for undue care of self in social relations, as there is (however persistently at present the vast majority of men overlook or fail to see the fact) for undue regard of self among the nations. We may mistakenly regard undue care of self in the body social as cleverness, aptitude for business, and so on; and we may mistakenly regard national selfishness as patriotism: but the process of evolution is as certainly working toward the elimination of one as of the other form of undue egoism.

The main condition of social welfare and of social progress is that the union which society implies shall work for the benefit of those associated. If the balance of effects resulting from association be evil, the body social must inevitably dissolve in the long run.

Now, by laws of greater or less severity the members of a race or nation may be compelled to recognize each others' claims. Or such recognition may be assured by the fear of retaliation if the claims of others are neglected. In such cases, however, the gain to each, or the egoistic advantage of association, is small. Enforced recognition of altruistic rights is in itself disagreeable. The more disagreeable it is the oftener will cases arise where the laws have to be called into operation (and their operation is by our supposition painful), or where retaliatory action is aroused, with waste of energy and disagreeable effects on either side. A society so restrained is held together by but weak bands, and is ill fitted to support itself against external enemies. Internal co-operation for the benefit of the community cannot be active under such circumstances. The products of labor are insecure. Moreover, whatever has to be done in the way of self-protection or of the safeguarding of property is so much withdrawn from the advancement of the general interests of the body social.

We have only to consider the condition of any European country, our own included, in the good old times which so many ignorant persons regret as a sort of golden age, to see how unsatisfactory must be the state of a nation in which only a stern code of laws, or the dread of retaliation, protects each against the undue egoism of his fellows. Internal wrong-doing and the necessity for constant struggle to resist such wrong-doing made each nation unstable. Our good old England was invaded and conquered over and over again in consequence of instability so produced. From long before the invasions by Saxon hordes under pirate chieftains to long after the invasion by Normans under the bastard descendant of the pirate chief Rollo, England was made wretched and miserable by constant contests, having their origin invariably in that undue egoism which we now call rapine and plunder. None—not even the most powerful—were secure. The castles we find so picturesque and romantic, the battles which seem glorious, the chivalry in which we see so much splendor, all tell us of a state of barbarism, of abject misery for the majority, of magnificent discomfort for the powerful. In the unsafety of those days, however, resided the certainty that the undue egoism of "the good old times" would by a natural process of evolution be eliminated. It is not yet fully eliminated; probably centuries will elapse before it is even in great part got rid of; but it is manifestly much reduced. We still have laws to protect us against wrong-doing, but the worst wrong-doers—those who of yore were the principal component parts of the body politic—no longer exist in the same way as of old. A much larger proportion of the social body recognize regard for others as a duty; no inconsiderable proportion recognize it as a pleasure; and, what is of more importance still, men recognize the advantage of encouraging these changed tendencies.

These changes have come on so gradually that few consider how important they really are. It is not too much to say that a large proportion of the Englishmen of our day would find life not worth living if the old state of things were restored; if, for instance, life and property and reputation became as insecure now as in the days of the Plantagenets, the Tudors, or even the Stuarts.

And here it may be noticed that those who neglect the consideration that they form part of the social body and refrain from the taking due part in maintaining a healthy social state suffer from the defective arrangements which they permit to remain uncorrected. We see this in very marked degree in America, though it can be recognized clearly—far too clearly—in our own country. There the best men keep out of politics for a reason which rightly understood should make all the best men take most anxious interest in politics. Because in America offices are too often filled by mere adventurers, because bribery and corruption are rife, and because fraudulent conduct is common among politicians, therefore should it be held the duty of every right-minded American to do his best to enforce the wholesome changes so obviously required—as they might be enforced if so many of the best Americans were duly altruistic. But as a matter of fact the very circumstance which should arouse all the best in America to vigorous action is made the chief reason for withdrawing from public duties.

In our own country the same undue egoism shows itself in another and a scarcely less mischievous form. The individual members of the community find relief in the thought that social duties may be handed over to government. It seems easier to talk laws into existence for getting things done than to do them. The laws are easily passed, but the doing of what is necessary passes in a great number of cases into the hands of men not nearly so much interested in the doing of it as those who passed the laws appointing them to the work—nay, often by the very nature of the laws so passed, interested rather in delaying than in pushing on the work.

As Mr. Spencer well puts it, the man who thus shirks the duties which he owes to the community of which he forms part, who plumes himself on his wisdom in minding his own business, "is blind to the fact that his own business is made possible only by maintenance of a healthy social state, and that he loses all round by defective governmental arrangements. When there are many likeminded with himself—when, as a consequence, offices come to be filled by political adventurers, and opinion is swayed by demagogues—when bribery vitiates the administration of the law and makes fraudulent state transactions habitual; heavy penalties fall on the community at large, and among others on those who have thus done everything for self and nothing for society. Their investments are insecure; recovery of their debts is difficult; and even their lives are less safe than they would otherwise have been. So that on such altruistic actions as are implied, firstly in being just, secondly in seeing justice done between others, and thirdly in upholding and improving the agencies by which justice is administered, depend, in large measure, the egoistic satisfactions of each."

Apart from dangers directly affecting life and property, those resulting from undue egoism in business relations show the necessity of just altruism for the welfare and happiness of the social body. Not only is it well for each to recognize the rights of others, but each is interested in securing due recognition of altruistic rights by his fellows. The evils resulting from business frauds affect the welfare of the community. To quote the illustrative cases cited by Mr. Spencer, "The larger the number of a shopkeeper's bills left unpaid by some customers, the higher must be the prices which other customers pay; the more manufacturers lose by defective raw materials or by carelessness of workmen, the more must they charge for their fabrics to buyers. The less trustworthy people are, the higher rises the rate of interest, the larger becomes the amount of capital hoarded, the greater are the impediments to industry; the further traders and people in general go beyond their means, and hypothecate the property of others in speculation, the more serious are those commercial panics which bring disasters on multitudes and injuriously affect all."—*Knowledge.*

IV

But we recognize the necessity of a more thorough altruism than that which merely considers the rights of others. That a community should progress as it ought, each member of the body social should feel that it is a part of his personal duty to consider the well-being of the rest. The weakness and the want of skill, the ill-health and the imperfect education of his fellows, are injurious to him and to all. In such degree as weakness or want of skill affects the productive power of some members of the community, the comfort and happiness of the stronger and more skillful are affected. The weak and inefficient members, who cannot provide for themselves, must be provided for somehow. The trouble to the community which would arise from any plan for leaving the weak and unskillful unprovided for would be much more serious than the loss arising from the efforts made to help them. But these efforts being so much deducted from the general efforts of the stronger and more skillful members of the body social must be counted as loss. So that it is the interest of all to see that there may be as few weak and unskillful persons in the community as possible.

In like manner the sickness of our fellows is a matter in which we are interested. Apart from the necessity of restoring the sick to such health and strength as may fit them to take their part in the work of the community, the illness of others may bring illness to ourselves. Fever and pestilence, though they may first attack the weak, presently extend their attacks to those who had been strong. If even a man should feel no anxiety on his own account, those dear to him, those dependent on him, or those on whom perhaps he is in greater or less degree dependent, may succumb to such attacks. Considering all the evils, near and remote, which may follow from an epidemic, we recognize the necessity of adopting all such altruistic measures as may avail to diminish the chance of such diseases arising, or to limit their range of action when they have once found footing. No doubt egoistic considerations here seem to suggest altruistic duties; but these altruistic duties cannot be properly undertaken or discharged unless they have become habitual and are referred to a real care and regard for others independently of consequences, more or less remote, to self. Apart from which, the discharge of such altruistic duties will be more satisfying and more pleasant if they are spontaneously undertaken.

Similar considerations apply to education in all its various forms. In other words, we must consider the mental as well as bodily weaknesses, and the mental as well as bodily diseases, of our fellow-citizens. "Where those around us are stupid and unintelligent, where they attempt no improvements, where they have little inventive capacity and little readiness to use even such as they have, we suffer along with them. The mere stupidity of the great mass of most communities with regard to the system of government they consent to be ruled by may mean most serious injury and discomfort to all, foolish and intelligent alike. Those who see what is needed, or at least the direction in which improvement may reasonably be sought, yet remain silent in the belief that it is no business of theirs, are as unintelligent as those who stupidly assent to what—without thinking—they suppose to be good for them and to be provided for by those who know better than themselves; though often, when traced to their source, the measures in vogue are found to be of no better origin than the body itself which submits to them.

A low standard of intelligence in the community affects the welfare of all, in many different ways. Wrong ideas about the relation of the nation to other nations may seem unimportant in the case of persons who take no direct part in political matters.

But in reality a very notable influence is exerted by the community generally on the conduct of those who have charge of political affairs. Wrong counsels in the cabinet may be advanced or right counsels hampered by stupidity in the country at large. Statesmen themselves are not always so wise or often so firm that they are not influenced by prevalent ideas; and so far as mere numbers are concerned prevalent ideas are likely to be foolish ideas. Fortunately, mere numbers may not suffice to give weight to prevalent stupidity. Many of the unwise are influenced by the observed fact that such and such men conduct affairs successfully, and so are led to support the wiser sort, not through sound judgment on their own part, but from that kind of sense which leads the ignorant to defer to the judgment of the better-informed. But this does not prevent the average intelligence of the community from being a matter of great moment even in political matters—supposed to be guided always by the wisest, despite the true saying that the world is governed with but a small amount of wisdom. What I have here said has no relation to the action of kings, princes, and the like, who in English-speaking communities cannot now injuriously influence political relations except through the weakness or folly of statesmen. Yet the argument might be strengthened by calling attention to the way in which, even within the last thirty years, our own country has suffered in this special direction, statesmen weakly or foolishly yielding to public pressure by which the unwise counsels of princes have been supported, A hundred years ago our country saw in still more marked way how the average want of intelligence of the many, supporting the stupidity of a king (of alien race, in that case), may go near to wreck the fortunes of a great race. We may hope, however, that no such trouble is in store for us hereafter as afflicted the British people when a foolish people insanely strengthened the hands of a mad king.

In social matters a low standard of general intelligence is a serious evil, which a wise altruism will endeavor to diminish. *"I do not mean,"* I may here say with Mr. Herbert Spencer, *"such altruism as taxes rate-payers that children's minds may he filled with dates and names and gossip about kings and narratives of battles and other useless information, no amount of which will make them capable workers or good citizens; but I mean such altruism as helps to spread a knowledge of the nature of things, and to cultivate the power of applying that knowledge."*

It is hardly necessary to multiply examples. We are confronted at every step by the harmful effects of prevalent want of intelligence. The fire which is intended to warm your room is so stupidly placed that it sends the better part of the heat up the chimney and creates cold draughts round your legs. Equally obnoxious to the understanding is the window by which you seek to ventilate your room. It is a struggle to open it, a struggle to close it, unless when your head is in the way, when it generally descends in effective guillotine-fashion. The carpeting of your room is an absurdity, the papering (apart from any question of beauty) a monstrosity. The gaseliers are so ingeniously arranged that you get a minimum of light and a maximum of heat and foul air. The chair you sit on seems intended to make you uncomfortable; as you draw it up to the table you find that the senseless people who plan furniture have provided sharp comers just where your knees are most likely to be caught. If you wish to lie down or to recline on a sofa, you find the head of the sofa so ingeniously padded that, while too sloped for reclining, it is not sloped enough for you to lie on it comfortably. Your child, running in for a kiss from papa, stumbles over a footstool so carefully colored like the carpet that it did not catch his eyes but his feet; and, falling, is hurt severely by a sharp projection on chair, sofa, table-leg, fender, scuttle, or what not, where no sharp projections are wanted, and none ever should be. In numberless ways miseries, individually small, but effectively diminishing happiness, result from general want of intelligence. "Unpunctuality and want of system," again, as Mr. Herbert Spencer points out, "are perpetual sources of annoyance. The unskillfulness of the cook causes frequent vexation and occasional indigestion. Lack of forethought in a house-maid leads to a fall over a bucket in a dark passage; and inattention to a message, or forgetfulness in delivering it, entails failure in an important engagement."

It is thus the interest of each one of us, and being also for the good of all becomes the duty of each, to be altruistic in regard to the mental progress of the community—"we benefit egoistically by such altruism as aids in raising the average intelligence."

But we are equally interested in the improvement of the moral feeling pervading the social body. The happiness of the whole community is diminished by the prevalence of unconscientious ways. In small matters as in large the principle prevails. We are all interested in helping to teach men the duty of considering the rights and claims of others. From the man who hustles others off the pavement or occupies an unfair share of what should be general conversation, to the man who swindles by gross aggressions or serious breach of contract, the products of a state of low average morality diminish the happiness of the community. The aggregate of discomfort wrought by paltry offenses is serious though each separate offense may produce but slight mischief. Moreover, offenses paltry in themselves may produce very serious results. The disobedience of a nurse in some small matter (such as taking her charge to this or that place) may lead to accident affecting life or limb, or to disease ending in permanent injury or in death. In other ways, mischievous results of greater or less importance are brought about by defective moral sense in small matters, while, when we consider the effects of want of conscientiousness in business, we recognize still more clearly how much we are all concerned in the moral improvement of the community. "Yesterday," says Mr. Herbert Spencer, "the illness of a child due to foul gases led to the discovery of a drain that had become choked because it was ill-made by a dishonest builder under supervision of a careless or bribed surveyor. Today workmen employed to rectify it occasion cost and inconvenience by dawdling, and their low standard of work, determined by the unionist principle that the better workers must not discredit the worse by exceeding them in efficiency, he may trace to the immoral belief" (well put!) "that the unworthy should fare as well as the worthy. To-morrow it turns out that business for the plumber has been provided by damage which the bricklayers have done." And so daily and hourly do we feel that the moral imperfections of the community are fit subjects for such altruistic efforts as may help to raise the average morality.

While we thus recognize that our well-being depends so greatly on the well-being of others—their health and bodily capacities, their sense and knowledge, and their moral qualities—that due regard for others is essential to the happiness of self, we see further that each member of the body social gains directly by the possession and exercise of such qualities as lead or enable him to help his fellows. Among the proverbs which present in brief the ideas of a race as to what is good and bad, are many which imply that regard for the interest and welfare of others is bad policy. Such proverbs cannot be regarded as expressing "the wisdom of many" by "the wit of one," for experience proves abundantly that the policy of hardness and indifference is unwise and short-sighted. Even mere material success—which does not always mean happiness—is not advanced in the longrun by disregard of others. The man of business gains in unnumbered ways by consideration for the rights and interests of his fellow-workers, and loses in as many by selfish disregard for them. Nay, even in the trivial affairs of ordinary life, at home and abroad, the kindly and considerate gain constantly, while the careless and indifferent as constantly suffer. It is, however, when we consider happiness as distinguished from mere material success, and the general balance of comfort and enjoyment as distinguished from the effects of individual actions, that we see how much men gain by sympathetic and kindly, conduct. We see even first-rate abilities and untiring energy beaten easily in the race of life by the kindliness which makes friends of all around and leads to opportunities which the hard and ungenial fail to obtain. But when we rightly apprehend the nature of life, and what makes life worth living, we find the chief gain of the kindly, not in these material opportunities, but in the pleasanter ways along which their life's work leads them. Compare two men, toward the evening of life, of whom both perhaps have achieved a fair amount of material success in life, but one of hard, unkindly manners, the other genial and sympathetic; one alone in life's struggle, the other with "troops of friends" from first to last. Who can doubt, as he compares the worn and weary look of one with the bright and cheerful aspect of the other, that regard for others counts for something toward the welfare and the happiness of self?

Care for others helps so surely in life's struggle that it would be good policy for the naturally hard man to benefit others for purely selfish motives, and still better policy to cultivate kindliness and consideration as qualities sure to be fruitful of profit. The kindly nature which leads to spontaneous good-will toward others, independently of any consideration of gain to self, is even more profitable than cultivated kindliness. Those are lucky who possess such a nature—lucky rather than deserving of special credit, seeing that a sympathetic nature is born in a man, not made by culture. Yet the will has much to do with the development of kindliness; and many, by sensible reflection and constant watchfulness over the undue promptings of self, have trained themselves to a kindliness and geniality of manner such as they were not naturally gifted with, and this without any direct reference to self-interest, but as a matter of right and justice to their fellows. Such men deserve much credit for their care in correcting inherent tendencies to undue care of self. The increased happiness of their lives (in so far at least as happiness depends on conduct) is their reward.

Among the good effects of kindly regard for others we may note the reflected happiness derived from those around. Men vary with their company, and undoubtedly the man of sympathetic temperament whose presence is a pleasure to others finds others much pleasanter in their relations with him than they would be were he of hard, ungenial nature. The wife and children of the kindly man are a constant pleasure to him, where the wife and children of the sour-tempered, ungenial husband and father are apt to grow gloomy and quarrelsome. His friends and relatives are kindlier than those of the harsh and selfish. Abroad, he sees few faces which do not reflect something of his own brightness and cheerfulness. As Mr. Herbert Spencer well says: "Such a one is practically surrounded by a world of better people than one who is less attractive: if we contrast the state of a man possessing all the material means to happiness, but isolated by his absolute egoism, with the state of an altruistic man relatively poor in means but rich in friends, we may see that various gratifications not to be purchased by money come in abundance to the last, and are inaccessible to the first."

But in yet other ways do we find illustrated by the effects of due care for others the saying, "To him that hath shall be given, and from him that hath not shall be taken even that which he seemeth to have."

Not only has the hard and ungenial man fewer gratifications, but those which he has he enjoys less than the man who cares for the wants and wishes of others. The one loses the power of enjoyment through his over-anxiety for self-gratification, the other unconsciously pursues—through his kindliness of character—the very course which a wise and thoughtful consideration of the plan best qualified to secure self-gratification would suggest. The one, while caring unduly for himself, is exhausting and satiating his power to care for any form of pleasure, the other while ministering to the enjoyments of others is fostering his own capacity for enjoyment. Here again, if one wished to suggest a course of action by which a man who suffered from life-weariness might again know the charm of happiness, one could advise no better course than to minister systematically to the enjoyments of those around. The very tide of life is made fuller thus, even as the tide of thought is made fuller by turning from mere reflection to a interchange of ideas and thoughts with those around. While there is work to be done in the way of increasing others' happiness, no man—not even the most jaded and satiated—need ask himself the sickly question, "Is life worth living?"

Especially is this so when the tide of life is ebbing. Mr. Spencer's words on this point are worthy of careful study, by those in particular who know of him only as the teacher of some hard, unsympathetic system of Gradgrindian philosophy, for they afford an apt example of his kindly and lovable teaching:

"It is in maturity and old age that we especially see how, as egoistic pleasures grow faint, altruistic actions come in to revive them in new forms. The contrast between the child's delight in the novelties daily revealed and the indifference which comes as the world around grows familiar, until in adult life there remain comparatively few things that are greatly enjoyed, draws from all the reflection that as years go by pleasures pall. And, to those who think, it becomes clear that only through sympathy can pleasures be indirectly gained from things that have ceased to yield pleasures directly. In the gratifications derived by parents from the gratifications of their offspring, this is conspicuously shown. Trite as is the remark that men live afresh in their children, it is needful here to set it down as reminding us of the way in which, as the egoistic satisfactions in life fade, altruism renews them while it transfigures them."

But not only does altruism increase the pleasures of life; the exercise of the altruistic qualities is in itself pleasurable. The state of mind when kindly actions are performed affords pleasure. It directly increases happiness, and thus (like other pleasures) enhances physical well-being. It is true that a sympathetic nature suffers where a hard and callous nature would feel no pain. Undue altruism has no doubt its bad effects, nor can it be denied that even such altruistic feelings as are desirable for the social well-being cause, at times, some degrees of suffering; but the exercise of the altruistic qualities is in the main pleasurable, and it cannot be doubted that altruistic emotions give more pleasure than sorrow. When we sorrow for a friend's grief we experience pain and undergo such depression of the vital functions as always accompanies pain; but in the long-run the joy felt in sympathy with the joys of others surpasses the sorrow occasioned by their troubles.

Then, too, it must be remembered that those pleasures which we derive from the arts owe a large part of their value to altruistic emotions. Consider the pleasure given by a painting representing a scene which moves our sympathies, or the delight with which we read some work of fiction in which kindly emotions are dealt with, and it will be seen how large a portion of our æsthetic gratifications depend on our sympathy with others. The hard and selfish care little for art and nothing for fiction. How should we bear to lose the pleasures which painting and sculpture, music and fiction, afford us? How even should we bear to change the pleasures given by the kindly and sympathetic art of to-day for the harsher effects of the arts of harder times when only deeds of conquest or ceremonial observances were represented in paintings and sculptures, suggested in musical strains, or recited in story or in song? What material gains, what sensual gratifications, what power, wealth, or fame, would make up (to us) for the pleasure we derive from the higher emotions? and how largely do these depend on the sympathies by which men are moved to loving care for the well-being of their fellows!

It remains lastly to be noticed that as there should be thought for others, and for the just rights and interests of others in the family, in the society with which we are directly associated, and within the race or nation, so there should be a wider altruism having regard to the rights of other races and nations. Hitherto men have scarcely at all recognized this duty. Very gradually the sense of altruistic duty passed beyond the family to the community of families, and thence still widening to the nation formed of such communities. Men learned that as personal selfishness is in the long-run opposed to the true interests of self, so family selfishness is only a degree less pernicious. The selfishness of parochialism was in turn seen to be mischievous, though it is still prevalent enough. But the selfishness of what is called patriotism—though it is as unlike true patriotism as personal selfishness is unlike due and wise self-regard—still remains as a virtue in the minds of most men, though characterized by inherent defects akin to those which belong to personal, family, and parochial selfishness. Men fail, indeed, to recognize any selfishness in undue care for what is called a man's own country—though with but vague and indefinite meaning. Nay, a blind love of country is regarded as something so directly the converse of selfishness, that Sir Walter Scott speaks of the absence of this sort of patriotism as simple selfishness. After asking if the man lives with soul so dead as never to have said to himself, "This is my own, my native land?" he goes on to say that such a man, a "wretch concentered all in self," can be swelled by no minstrel music, and is bound to go unmourned and unsung to an unhonored grave. The idea that patriotism could under any circumstances be exaggerated, and become but a widened form of selfishness, would doubtless have outraged utterly Scott's sense of the fitness of things. Yet viewing matters from the outside, and, as far as possible, independently of inbred ideas, there is nothing except its wider range to distinguish the selfishness of exaggerated patriotism from personal or family selfishness.

That patriotic selfishness is mischievous in its effects would scarcely need showing if men were not so ready as they are to be deaf to the teachings of experience. The well-being of other nations is in the same sense essential to the well-being of our own nation as the well-being of other members of the body social is essential to our own personal well-being. The misfortunes of any nation with which our own has relations are misfortunes to our own nation, however they may be brought about, whether by internal misgovernment, by the attacks of other nations, or by our own warlike measures. There can be no doubt, for example, that the loss incurred by Germany, the victor, was only less than the loss incurred by France, the conquered, in the disastrous Franco-German War. Other nations suffered greatly, but Germany more, and France most of all. In the war with Russia, in 1854-'55, all Europe suffered. In the American civil war not only all the United States but the whole world incurred loss. It is easy for nations to blind themselves, nay, most nations are naturally blind, to the losses suffered by each through the misfortunes of others. But there can be no doubt about the actual facts. The British race would have been taught the lesson long since, if the lesson could reach the average national mind through experience—for we are suffering, have long been suffering, and long must suffer, from the energetic efforts of our "imperial" race to get the better of other races. Directly and indirectly, in loss of blood and material, in the paralysis of trade as well as in increased expenditure, our people has to pay for its imperial instincts, just as the man of over-bearing, hard, and selfish nature has to pay in many ways for the gratification of his instincts imperious. There are the same reasons, based on material profit, for inculcating just and considerate dealings between peoples as there are for encouraging just and considerate dealings between man and man. But at present nations delight in proclaiming themselves selfish and overbearing; the more brutal instincts which remain dominant in nations after they have begun to die out in individuals are upheld as virtues, much as in old times many races regarded the more brutal qualities of humanity as chief among the virtues.—*Knowledge.*

Conclusion

It remains only now that I should consider the general conclusions toward which our discussion of the subject of happiness as a guide to conduct may appear to have led us.

Let me note, yet once more, that those have entirely misapprehended the whole drift of this series of papers who imagine, as many still seem to do, that my subject has been the morality of being happy, the propriety of seeking after happiness. The mistake appears so absurd, when the nature of the reasoning I have advanced is considered, that it would seem hardly worth while to correct it, seeing that no one who could fall into such a mistake could (one would imagine) in the least profit by any explanation or correction. Yet the mistake has been made by several who are clearly not devoid of capacity alike to render and to receive a reason. I have, therefore, felt bound to correct it as far as possible, and, as several letters recently received show that the error is still entertained, I have now to correct it afresh. Let me explain, then, that the object of these papers has been to show what sort of moral law is likely to arise, and what law appears actually to have arisen and to be in progress of formation, when the guide of conduct is the increase of happiness—individual happiness, and the happiness of those around us, with due regard to the proper apportionment of altruistic and egoistic happiness. I have not examined such questions as. What is happiness? What kind of happiness is worthiest? and so forth. I have taken, as included in the term "happiness," all the various forms of pleasurable emotion of which the human race is susceptible, while all the various forms of painful emotion to which we are exposed have come naturally into consideration as all involving greater or less diminution of happiness. With the development of the human race, or of any part of the human race, in one direction or in another (for development is multiform), we find that ideas about pleasure and pain become modified in various ways. And it has been a special part of our subject to consider how the lower forms of pleasure, those related first to the physical gratification of self, and next those related specially to self but otherwise of higher type, give place gradually to the higher gratifications arising from altruistic relations. But, apart from such considerations, our whole inquiry has been into the development of conduct by the natural operation of those laws which influence the development of happiness.

In passing I would, however, note that the law of conduct thus considered is by no means that abstraction which has been called "the happiness of the greater number," according to which each person is to regard himself and to be regarded as one, while the rest, being many, are to be regarded as of very much greater importance. This abstraction has not and never had any value whatever, as a rule of conduct, either in a man's self or in his relation to others. Even if we can adopt any meaning for the word happiness as thus used, it will be found that no rational way of apportioning the happiness thus regarded as a sort of common property, can be conceived. If the law instead of being an abstraction were real and could be definitely applied, it could result only in this, that each person, being but one, should utterly neglect his individual welfare in favor of the general happiness, and, as it can be readily seen that no benefits he might receive from those around him (obeying, we may assume, the same law) could possibly compensate for the direct and immediate effects of this complete self-abnegation, it follows that a community of persons obeying this law would be a community of miserable beings; so that obedience to this law for obtaining general happiness would in reality insure universal misery.

Taking concrete instead of abstract happiness as the guide of conduct, were cognize far different results. We see that, though there must of necessity be a compromise between egoistic satisfactions and altruistic cares, the compromise need by no means imply antagonism. Regard for the welfare of others, though in its inception more or lass of an effort, becomes more and more spontaneous as social relations develop. After spontaneity has been attained, altruistic actions involve more and more of egoistic satisfaction. Conversely, the care of self, which in the earlier stages of social development appears to involve more or less of disregard for the interests of others, becomes more and more altruistic in its effect as society advances. Thus also we recognize the answer to what at first might seem a difficulty, viz., that with the improvement of social relations the opportunity for altruistic actions might seem likely to steadily diminish. We see that the domain available for altruistic actions changes in position rather than in extent; nay, that such change of extent as actually accrues is toward increase. In a society where, owing to the steady improvement of the relation between egoistic and altruistic interests, the number of those depending for their happiness or even for their existence on altruistic cares has steadily diminished, the number of those who are the subject of altruistic emotions will as steadily have increased. Sympathy becomes more widely extended, its development becomes surer and more rapid, as its operation becomes more pleasurable, and a change of this sort cannot but take place as occasions for directly altruistic actions, such as arise out of pain and suffering, become less frequent.

With increased spontaneity in altruistic actions, more pleasurable feelings in the discharge of altruistic duties, and a wider range for altruistic emotions, will inevitably come such an evolution of conduct as must tend greatly to increase the well-being of the community. The care of self will be felt as a duty to others; due care of others will become a source of gratification to self. Society will be simply, on an enlarged scale and in a more varied form, such a community as might be formed by a number of kindly, well-meaning persons, of good capacity and pleasing manners, brought together for purposes of travel, research, or pleasure. In such a community it would be felt that each person's first duty was to take due care of self, first as just to himself, and secondly (yet chiefly) as a duty to the rest of the community. But it would also be felt by each member of such a community that he must be careful of the interests of others, ready to be of use to any other members of the community who required assistance such as he could give individually, or to combine with others where the assistance of several might seem to be required. Picture the relations of such a community, all of good-will, kindly, and anxious that the business of the community should go on so as to give pleasure to all, and it will be at once seen how little there is of actual selfishness in due care of self, how such care may be, nay, must be, a duty owed to all the rest; while, on the other hand, it will become clear also how each member of such a community is interested in the existence among all of a kindly interest on the part of each in the well-being of the rest. The social body, whether we consider the family, or the gathering of families into communities, or the collection of communities into nations, or the multitude of nations which form the population of the earth, may be regarded as an aggregate which should be pervaded by such ideas as are found essential for the comfort and happiness of gatherings casually brought together. The due subordination of self to others in certain relations, and of others to self in relations not less important, which is found in all such gatherings on a small scale and of comparatively uniform character—as in the passengers on an ocean-steamship, the members of a company of travelers, the fellows of a scientific expedition, or even a pleasure-party—is what is necessary for the well-being of the body social; and out of this necessity, instinctively recognized, and exercising its influence steadily in the process of the evolution of races, nations, and the human family as a whole, seem to have sprung all those duties between man and man, between race and race, and between nation and nation, which form the present code of social morals, and will hereafter—developed and improved—form the moral code of perfected man. "What now, in even the highest natures," as the great teacher of our day says, "is occasional and feeble may be expected with further evolution to become habitual and strong; and what now characterizes the exceptionally high may be expected eventually to characterize all. For that which the best human nature is capable of is within the reach of human nature at large."

"That these conclusions," Mr. Spencer goes on to say, "will meet with any considerable acceptance is improbable. Neither with current ideas nor with current sentiments are they sufficiently congruous. Such a view will not be agreeable to those who lament the spreading disbelief in eternal damnation; nor to those who follow the apostle of brute force in thinking that because the rule of the strong hand was once good it is good for all time; nor to those whose reverence for one who told them to put up the sword is shown by using the sword to spread his doctrine among heathens." From ten thousand teachers of a religion of love who are silent when a nation is moved by the religion of hate will come no sign of assent; nor from those priestly lawgivers who, "far from urging the extreme precept of the Master they pretend to follow, to turn the other cheek when one is smitten, vote for acting on the principle. Strike lest ye be struck. Nor will any approval be felt by legislators who, after praying to be forgiven their trespasses as they forgive the trespasses of others, forthwith decide to attack those who have not trespassed against them. But though men who profess Christianity and practice Paganism can feel no sympathy with such a view, there are some, classed as antagonists to the current creed, who may not think it absurd to believe that a rationalized version of its ethical principles will eventually be acted upon."

Finally, I would ask those who have followed me thus far to note how all the duties we have considered, both egoistic duties and altruistic ones, may be seen with advantage from a different point of view and in a changed aspect, though unchanged in reality. We are in the habit of regarding the study of moral laws always from the personal side, and nearly all teachers in such matters (one might almost say all) view the subject in this way, since, even when laying down a code of morals, they present each law as it appeals to the reason and should affect the conduct of the individual. But it should be remembered that a moral law which commends to each man a particular line of conduct, is a law which, if accepted and followed by all, influences each man by the effect it produces on all the rest. Thus, a rule of conduct seemingly egoistic, and really egoistic as affecting the individual, becomes, in any society which accepts and obeys it, purely altruistic in its effect; while, *per contra*, a law seemingly altruistic in terms becomes purely egoistic in influence. If, instead of indicating a due regard for self and a proper subordination of self to others, our study of the morality of happiness had indicated as best for the community a series of duties directed solely to the benefit of self, yet the adoption of such a moral code by all men would be altogether unselfish, seeing that it would mean the forsaking of all right or title to help or sympathy from others; and others are many, while self is but one. If, on the other hand, we had found a system of perfect altruism commending itself as best, the acceptance of such a system would be no sacrificing of self to others, but would mean the acceptance of the principle that everyone else was bound to assist in all his ways and wishes the accepter of this seemingly altruistic code—to sympathize with him in all his sorrows, and to care for him far more than for themselves. We have not been led to recognize any such abnegation of self on the one hand, or regard for self alone on the other hand, as desirable; but, in such degree as we have seen a regard for self to be desirable, we have in reality been led to the recognition of the rights of others (since each self is another to all others), while, in such degree as we have seen that each should consider not only the rights but the requirements of others, we have been led in reality to the recognition of the rights of each man to the assistance and sympathy of his fellows.

www.ingramcontent.com/pod-product-compliance
Lightning Source LLC
Chambersburg PA
CBHW031402040426
42444CB00005B/393